The History of France

Crafted by Skriuwer

Copyright © 2024 by Skriuwer.

All rights reserved. No part of this book may be used or reproduced in any form whatsoever without written permission except in the case of brief quotations in critical articles or reviews.

At **Skriuwer**, we're more than just a team—we're a global community of people who love books. In Frisian, "Skriuwer" means "writer," and that's at the heart of what we do: creating and sharing books with readers worldwide. Wherever you are in the world, **Skriuwer** is here to inspire learning.

Frisian is one of the oldest languages in Europe, closely related to English and Dutch, and is spoken by about **500,000 people** in the province of **Friesland** (Fryslân), located in the northern Netherlands. It's the second official language of the Netherlands, but like many minority languages, Frisian faces the challenge of survival in a modern, globalized world.

We're using the money we earn to promote the Frisian language.

For more information, contact : **kontakt@skriuwer.com** (www.skriuwer.com)

TABLE OF CONTENTS

Chapter 1: Prehistoric France And The Arrival Of Early Societies

- *Early Human Settlement And Archaeological Findings*
- *Transition From Hunter-Gatherers To Neolithic Farming*
- *Megalithic Monuments And Iron Age Tribal Development*

Chapter 2: The Gauls, Greek Colonies, & The Roman Conquest

- *Celtic Tribes, Greek Trading Posts, And Cultural Exchange*
- *Julius Caesar's Campaigns And The Romanization Of Gaul*
- *Formation Of Roman Provinces And The Beginnings Of Gallo-Roman Culture*

Chapter 3: Roman Gaul

- *Provinces, Roads, And Aqueducts Under Roman Rule*
- *Latin Language, Gallo-Roman Religion, And Urban Life*
- *Spread Of Christianity And Its Early Influence*

Chapter 4: The Fall Of Rome And The Rise Of The Franks

- *Decline Of Roman Authority And Barbarian Incursions*
- *Clovis's Unification Of Frankish Tribes*
- *Transition From Roman To Early Medieval Power Structures*

Chapter 5: The Merovingians And The Shaping Of Early Medieval France

- *Dynastic Struggles Among Merovingian Kings*
- *Role Of The Church And Monastic Centers*
- *Foundations Of Feudal Relationships And Noble Power*

Chapter 6: The Carolingian Dynasty And The Reign Of Charlemagne

- *Pepin The Short's Rise And Charlemagne's Consolidation*
- *Cultural Revival, Script Reform, And The Carolingian Renaissance*
- *Imperial Coronation And The Legacy Of Charlemagne*

Chapter 7: The Fragmentation Of Power And The Feudal System

- *Treaty Of Verdun And The Breaking Of Carolingian Unity*
- *Noble Lords, Knights, And Peasant Obligations*
- *Viking Raids And The Decentralization Of Authority*

Chapter 8: The Capetian Dynasty And The Growth Of Royal Authority

- *Hugh Capet's Election And The Early Capetian Kings*
- *Strengthening Of Royal Power, Administrative Reforms*
- *Alliances, Church Relations, And The Expansion Of The Royal Domain*

Chapter 9: The Hundred Years' War And Joan Of Arc

- *Conflict Between France And England Over Territorial Claims*
- *Key Battles, Military Evolutions, And Social Impacts*
- *Joan Of Arc's Leadership, Martyrdom, And National Symbolism*

Chapter 10: The Rise Of The Valois And The Consolidation Of Power

- *Recovery After The Hundred Years' War And Territorial Unification*
- *Centralization Efforts, Standing Armies, And Royal Finances*
- *Late Medieval Society And The Strengthening Of The Monarchy*

Chapter 11: The French Renaissance Under Francis I

- Humanist Scholarship, Court Patronage, And Artistic Flourishing
- Concordat Of Bologna And Royal Authority Over The Church
- Influence Of Italian Wars On Culture And Diplomacy

Chapter 12: The Wars Of Religion & The Reign Of Henry Iv

- Huguenot-Catholic Conflicts And The Emergence Of Religious Factions
- St. Bartholomew's Day Massacre And Its Lasting Impact
- Henry Iv's Edict Of Nantes And The Path To Religious Coexistence

Chapter 13: The Bourbon Dynasty & The Reign Of Louis Xiii

- Cardinal Richelieu's Centralizing Policies
- Suppression Of Huguenot Strongholds And Feudal Autonomy
- France's Intervention In The Thirty Years' War

Chapter 14: The Age Of Louis Xiv And Absolutism

- Versailles As A Symbol Of Royal Power And Court Culture
- The Revocation Of The Edict Of Nantes And Religious Uniformity
- Wars Of Expansion And The Final Strain On The Monarchy

Chapter 15: The Enlightenment And The Late Bourbon Era

- Rise Of Philosophes And Critical Thinking
- Financial Crises And Reform Failures Under Louis Xv And Louis Xvi
- Social Tensions And The Calling Of The Estates-General (1789)

Chapter 16: The French Revolution And The End Of The Monarchy

- Formation Of The National Assembly And The Storming Of The Bastille
- Radicalization, The Execution Of Louis Xvi, And Republican Experiments
- Wars With Europe And The Final Collapse Of The Old Regime

Chapter 17: The Rise And Fall Of Napoleon Bonaparte

- Napoleon's Coup Of 18 Brumaire And The Consulate
- Imperial Conquests, The Napoleonic Code, And Continental Dominance
- Russian Campaign Disaster And The Defeat At Waterloo

Chapter 18: The Restoration And The July Monarchy

- Return Of The Bourbon Kings And The Charter Of 1814
- Charles X's Ultra-Royalist Policies And The 1830 Revolution
- Louis-Philippe's "Bourgeois Monarchy" And Political Unrest

Chapter 19: The Second Empire And The Rise Of Nationalism

- Louis-Napoleon's Presidency, Coup D'état, And Proclamation As Emperor
- Haussmann's Renovation Of Paris, Industrial Growth, And Foreign Ventures
- Franco-Prussian War And The Downfall Of Napoleon Iii

Chapter 20: The Third Republic And France At The End Of The 19th Century

- Aftermath Of The War, The Paris Commune, And Republican Consolidation
- Dreyfus Affair, Church-State Separation, And Secular Education
- Social Reforms, Colonial Expansion, And The Shaping Of A Modern Republic

CHAPTER 1: PREHISTORIC FRANCE AND ARRIVAL OF EARLY SOCIETIES

Introduction

France's history begins far before the rise of famous kings and powerful empires. To understand how France became what it is, we need to explore the earliest signs of human life in the region. Prehistoric France is full of different ages, groups, and changes in lifestyle. This was a time long before written records, so we rely on archaeological findings like cave paintings, stone tools, and the remains of ancient campsites. In this chapter, we will look at how early humans arrived in the land that we now call France. We will also see how they adapted to changing environments and invented new ways of living.

Because there are no direct written records from these ancient people, historians and archaeologists have to look at fossils, artifacts, and the land itself to build a picture. Fossils give us clues about what kinds of humans lived in France. Tools tell us how they hunted or gathered food. And the remains of settlements show how they organized their communities. Although it is impossible to know everything about these distant times, each discovery helps us form a clearer understanding of the earliest history.

This chapter discusses the period before the Roman conquest. We will begin with the oldest traces of humans, move through the Paleolithic era, and then explore the Mesolithic, Neolithic, Bronze Age, and Iron Age. In doing so, we will see how small groups of hunters and gatherers eventually became settled farmers and, later, early metalworkers. We will pay attention to cave art, burial practices, and the development of social structures. By the end of this chapter, you will have a detailed view of the foundations of life in ancient France.

The Land Before People

Long before humans arrived, the land that is now France was shaped by geological forces like shifting continents, changing sea levels, and different climates. Millions of years ago, dinosaurs roamed parts of the region. Over time, tectonic activity formed mountain ranges such as the Pyrenees in the southwest and the Alps in the east. Major rivers like the Seine, the Loire, the Garonne, and the Rhone carved out their valleys, influencing where future human groups would travel and settle.

During the Ice Ages, large parts of Europe were covered by thick sheets of ice. Although most of France was not fully covered by glaciers, the colder climate pushed plants and animals to move south or adapt. When temperatures dropped, the landscape became more like tundra, with grasslands and sparse trees. As ice sheets retreated, the climate gradually warmed, allowing forests to spread again. These changes in the environment over thousands of years created varied habitats that supported different groups of animals.

Before people, great herds of mammals roamed these lands. Mammoths, woolly rhinoceroses, giant deer, and other large creatures were common sights. Predators like cave lions and bears followed the herds. The availability of game, along with streams and rivers full of fish, would later attract human hunter-gatherers to the region. Natural shelters, such as caves in limestone regions, offered protection from harsh weather. These geographical features set the stage for early human arrival, giving them resources and places to live.

Early Humans in France

Evidence of human presence in what is now France goes back hundreds of thousands of years. One of the oldest human species that left traces here was Homo heidelbergensis, which dates to about 600,000 years ago. Over time, this species evolved or was replaced by Neanderthals (Homo neanderthalensis), who thrived in many parts of Europe. Neanderthals were well-suited to cold climates and had strong bodies that helped them survive. They made use of stone tools, hunted large animals, and may have had some form of symbolic thinking.

Neanderthal sites in France, such as La Chapelle-aux-Saints and Le Moustier, reveal details about their lives. They left behind stone tools known for their distinctive shapes and craftsmanship. Some sites suggest that Neanderthals buried their dead or performed some kind of ritual, showing that they might have had spiritual or cultural practices. They created shelters near caves or rock overhangs and made use of fire for warmth and cooking.

Around 40,000 to 45,000 years ago, modern humans (Homo sapiens) began arriving in Europe. Commonly associated with the Aurignacian culture and later cultures like the Gravettian, these modern humans brought new tool-making techniques and different forms of art. Over time, they spread throughout France, coexisting for a while with Neanderthals and possibly competing for resources. By around 30,000 to 35,000 years ago, Neanderthals had disappeared, leaving modern humans as the dominant human species in France.

The Paleolithic Era

The Paleolithic era, or Old Stone Age, extends from the earliest stone tools made by human ancestors up to about 10,000 years ago. In France, this era is important for understanding how humans survived in often harsh climates. People lived in small, mobile groups. They hunted large mammals like mammoths, reindeer, and horses, and also gathered plants, fruits, and nuts. They followed migratory animal herds, moving their camps to where resources were abundant.

The development of stone tool technology was slow but steady. Early Paleolithic tools were large and simple. Over time, people learned to create sharper blades and more specialized implements, such as scrapers and points. They also made bone tools, like needles, which helped them sew animal skins into clothes. Surviving the cold required invention and cooperation. Groups likely shared knowledge of successful hunting strategies.

Many Paleoanthropologists note that Paleolithic communities in France varied from region to region depending on the local environment. Coastal regions provided fish and shellfish, while inland areas were more reliant on land-based animals. Caves, especially in southwestern France, became natural shelters. Archaeological sites like those in the Vézère Valley (including famous caves such as Lascaux) show evidence that these groups spent long periods of time in these areas.

Cave Art

One of the most remarkable features of Paleolithic life in France is the cave art. The walls of caves like Lascaux and Chauvet are decorated with vivid paintings that date back as far as 30,000 to 40,000 years. These paintings show animals like horses, bulls, deer, and sometimes more mysterious signs or human-like figures. The images often have detail and movement, suggesting a high level of skill and observation.

The question of why these early humans created cave art is still debated. Some think it had a spiritual or magical purpose, possibly related to hunting rituals. Others believe it might have served as a record of successful hunts, a way to teach hunting techniques, or a form of storytelling. The caves themselves can be quite deep and difficult to access, suggesting the art was not simply decoration for daily living spaces. Whatever their exact purpose, these paintings highlight the creative and symbolic abilities of early humans.

For archaeologists, cave art is a window into ancient thinking. Although we cannot know every meaning behind the images, we can see that these people cared about representing the animals they depended on. They used pigments made from minerals like ochre and charcoal, applying them with fingers, brushes, or by blowing the pigment through hollow bones or reeds to create a spray effect. The paintings show shading and the use of the cave's natural contours to add depth, proving an impressive artistic awareness.

Mesolithic Transition

Around 10,000 years ago, as the last Ice Age ended, the climate grew warmer and the environment changed. Large Ice Age animals either migrated north or became extinct. Forests spread across much of France, and new types of plants and animals became available. Humans entered a period called the Mesolithic, or Middle Stone Age.

During the Mesolithic, people adapted their hunting strategies to focus on smaller game like deer, boar, and fish. They also gathered plant foods, nuts, and berries from forests. Their tools became more specialized, with microliths—small, sharp stone pieces—attached to shafts or handles to make arrows, spears, and other composite tools. This shift from hunting big game in open plains to managing mixed forests and smaller game required flexibility and innovation.

Settlements also changed. Although people remained mobile, they sometimes formed seasonal camps near rivers and lakes to fish or collect shellfish. In coastal regions, shell middens—heaps of discarded shells—provide evidence of repeated use of these sites. Over time, longer stays in certain places may have led to increased social interaction between groups. While these Mesolithic communities still relied heavily on nature's offerings, they laid the groundwork for the more settled life of the Neolithic.

The Neolithic Revolution in France

The Neolithic era, or New Stone Age, began in different parts of Europe at different times, but in France it generally started around 6,000 to 5,000 BCE. The major change that defines the Neolithic is the shift from a hunter-gatherer lifestyle to one based on farming and animal husbandry. This shift was gradual and may have come from the spread of ideas and people from areas like the Near East, where agriculture was first developed.

Farming communities in France raised crops such as wheat and barley. They also domesticated animals like cattle, sheep, and goats. Permanent villages and houses made of wattle-and-daub or timber appeared, and with them, storage facilities for grain. Pottery became a key feature of Neolithic life. People used ceramic vessels to store food and water. The style and decoration of pottery varied by region and changed over time, giving archaeologists a way to track the spread of cultures.

Neolithic farmers could produce more reliable food supplies, allowing populations to grow. Over time, these farming communities developed more complex social structures. Some regions show signs of large communal projects, like building defensive walls or impressive monuments. This suggests leadership roles, group efforts, and possibly the beginnings of social hierarchies. The Neolithic era marks a fundamental transformation in how people lived, setting the stage for further development in France's prehistory.

Megalithic Sites and Monument Building

One of the most striking features of late Neolithic life in France is the construction of megalithic monuments. The word "megalithic" means "large stone," and these monuments include dolmens (stone tombs), menhirs (standing stones), and stone circles. Brittany, in the northwest of France, is famous for its dense clusters of megaliths, such as the alignments of Carnac. Some of these sites date to around 4500 BCE or even earlier, making them among the oldest standing stone structures in the world.

Why did these ancient people invest so much energy into moving and erecting huge stones? Scholars suggest many possibilities. Megaliths might have served religious or ceremonial purposes. They could be markers of territories or meeting places for different clans. Some megalithic tombs show evidence that they were used for collective burials over generations. This indicates a belief in shared ancestry or afterlife rituals.

Moving these stones, some weighing several tons, required coordinated effort, planning, and the use of log rollers or sleds. This level of organization points to increasingly complex social structures. In addition, the presence of large communal burial sites suggests that certain groups in society managed or led these building projects. By studying the orientation and arrangement of the stones, archaeologists also explore the possibility of early knowledge of astronomy or solar and lunar alignments.

The Bronze Age: Emergence of Metallurgy

As time progressed, human communities in France began to use metal, first copper and then bronze (an alloy of copper and tin). The Bronze Age in France started around 2000 BCE, although the exact date varies by region. Metal tools and weapons offered clear advantages over stone. They were stronger, more durable, and could be shaped into precise forms. This allowed for new agricultural tools like more effective axes and sickles, as well as better weapons like bronze swords and spears.

Societies that mastered metallurgy gained status and power. Trade networks emerged because not all regions had the raw materials for making bronze. Copper and tin had to be obtained from areas with mineral deposits, sometimes far away. These trade routes also brought ideas and cultural influences, spreading knowledge of metalworking and introducing new styles of pottery, jewelry, and other goods.

Towns and fortified settlements started to appear in strategic locations, often near metal resources or trade routes. This was a time when wealth and social stratification grew. Some individuals or families, who controlled metal sources or trade connections, held greater authority. Burial sites from the Bronze Age sometimes show clear differences in status, with wealthy graves containing metal tools, jewelry, and imported goods, while others contain simpler items. This evolving social complexity laid the groundwork for the later Iron Age and the development of powerful tribal cultures in Gaul.

The Iron Age

Following the Bronze Age, iron became the primary metal for tools and weapons. The Iron Age in France began around the 8th century BCE. Iron was more abundant than copper or tin, which made it easier for societies to obtain the raw materials needed to craft weapons and tools. This led to an expansion of farming, as iron plows could more effectively turn the soil, boosting food production. A steady food supply allowed populations to grow and tribes to form more stable settlements.

During the Iron Age, what we now refer to as Celtic culture spread widely in western and central Europe. In the area that became France, these Celtic-speaking people are often called Gauls (though the term Gauls will be discussed more fully in the next chapter). They lived in various tribal groups, each with its own territories, leaders, and customs. Archaeological sites from this period show advanced metalwork, pottery, and even the use of coinage in some places.

By the late Iron Age, large fortified settlements called oppida developed. These were more than just defensive sites; they served as centers for trade, craftsmanship, and governance. The remains of walls, gates, and planned streets show that these communities were organized and could coordinate building projects. Tribal elites displayed their power through lavish burials, complete with fine metal objects, imported luxury items, and sometimes even war chariots. These signs of wealth and organization point to the growing complexity of societies in ancient France, setting the stage for interaction and, eventually, conflict with the expanding Roman Empire.

Shifting Societies and the Threshold of History

By the end of the prehistoric era and moving into the Iron Age, the region that would become France was not a single political unit but rather a patchwork of different tribal groups. Each group had its own culture and leaders, and they sometimes cooperated or fought with their neighbors. Trade brought outside influences from the Mediterranean, especially from Greek and Etruscan traders, and these influences introduced new ideas and goods.

Written records in this period are minimal and mostly come from outside observers, like Greek merchants who described the peoples of the western Mediterranean. True written history in France begins to emerge more clearly with the arrival of the Romans, who produced extensive records. But the roots of French history lie in these long prehistoric periods. Over tens of thousands of years, humans in France moved from simple hunter-gatherer groups to organized tribes capable of building large fortifications, trading over long distances, and creating complex societies.

In this chapter, we have traced the path of early human development in France, from the days of Neanderthals through the Paleolithic, Mesolithic, Neolithic, Bronze Age, and Iron Age. Each stage brought new technologies, social changes, and cultural expressions. Cave art, megalithic monuments, metalworking, and fortified settlements all left their mark on the landscape. These foundations prepared the region for the significant transformations that would come with increasing contact with the classical civilizations of the Mediterranean. Next, we will explore how Celtic tribes, Greek colonies, and the Roman Republic changed this land forever.

CHAPTER 2: THE GAULS, GREEK COLONIES, AND THE ROMAN CONQUEST

Introduction

By the time we reach the Iron Age, the region we call France was home to many tribes often referred to collectively as Gauls. They shared similar Celtic languages and cultural traits, but they were by no means a single, united people. At the same time, Greek merchants and colonists had begun to establish trading posts along the Mediterranean coast, shaping local economies and introducing new ideas. Eventually, the Romans turned their eyes to Gaul, seeing it as both a threat (especially after occasional raids into Roman territory) and a land of opportunity with rich farmlands and resources.

In this chapter, we will explore the complex social fabric of the Gauls, the influence of Greek colonies, and the gradual shift that brought the region under Roman control. We will pay special attention to major figures and events, such as the famous general Julius Caesar and the Gallic chieftain Vercingetorix. These developments mark a turning point in French history. The once loosely connected tribal societies would be reshaped into a province of the Roman Empire. This transformation laid many of the foundations for what would later become medieval France.

Celtic Culture and the Gauls

The term "Gauls" generally refers to the Celtic-speaking peoples who lived in what is now France (as well as parts of Belgium, Switzerland, northern Italy, and other regions). Over centuries, these tribes developed distinct customs, social structures, and religions. They were skilled ironworkers, producing strong and effective tools and weapons. Gaulish art included intricate patterns, stylized animal motifs, and decorative metalwork.

Tribal Organization

The Gauls did not form a single state. Instead, they lived in multiple tribes with their own leaders and internal structures. Some tribes were quite large and organized, controlling territories dotted with small settlements and oppida (fortified towns). Each tribe had a chief or a king, sometimes advised by councils of elders or warrior elites. Alliances, feuds, and shifting coalitions were part of daily political life.

Economy and Trade

Iron Age Gaul had a mixed economy based on farming, livestock breeding, and craft production. Surplus grain, livestock, and manufactured goods like textiles and metal items were traded within Gaul and with neighboring regions. Trade routes connected the tribes to the Mediterranean world, where they could exchange raw materials such as metals and furs for luxury goods like wine, pottery, and jewelry. Over time, some Gaulish elites grew wealthy from these exchanges, adopting some Mediterranean customs and goods to show their status.

Religion and Druids

One notable aspect of Gaulish society was the presence of druids, who served as religious leaders, teachers, and sometimes political advisors. The druids oversaw rituals, judged disputes, and preserved oral traditions. They were highly respected and often above the warrior class in status. The Celtic religion involved many gods and goddesses linked to nature, such as deities of the sun, the rivers, and the harvest. Sacred groves, springs, and other natural sites had great spiritual importance.

Greek Colonies in Southern Gaul

While the interior of Gaul was dominated by Celtic tribes, the southern coast saw the arrival of Greek settlers as early as the 6th century BCE. The Greeks from cities like Phocaea (in Asia Minor) sailed west, establishing trade outposts and eventually forming permanent colonies. One of the most famous was Massalia (modern-day Marseille), founded around 600 BCE.

Massalia and Its Influence

Massalia grew into a significant port city. Greek settlers brought their language, art, coinage, and knowledge of shipbuilding and navigation. This city-state became a hub for trade between the Mediterranean and the interior of Gaul. Goods like metals, grain, and even slaves passed through its harbor. In return, local tribes received Greek pottery, wine, and other luxury items. Massalia's influence extended along the coast, with smaller Greek enclaves forming in nearby areas.

Cultural Exchange

The presence of the Greeks led to cultural exchange. Some Gaulish elites learned aspects of Greek culture, from writing systems to architectural ideas. Greek pottery styles influenced local craft traditions. The combination of Greek merchants and Gallic trading partners produced a blending of traditions. Certain Gaulish coins began to carry Greek-inspired designs or inscriptions. This shows how tribes near Greek colonies adopted outside ideas, often merging them with their own Celtic traditions.

Alliances and Conflicts

As Massalia became wealthier, it had to defend itself against rival tribes and other groups who wanted to control its lucrative trade. The city sometimes formed alliances with certain Gallic tribes, offering them benefits in exchange for protection. The relationship between Greeks and Gauls was not always peaceful, but the trade connections were valuable enough that both sides usually tried to maintain a workable coexistence.

Early Roman Interest in Gaul

Rome's relationship with Gaul began with trade and occasional military encounters. Some Gaulish raids crossed the Alps into Italy, causing alarm among the Romans. Over time, the Romans pushed northward, first gaining control over the region of Cisalpine Gaul (roughly northern Italy). They also formed alliances with Greek cities like Massalia, appreciating their strategic coastal positions.

Roman Province of Gallia Narbonensis

In 125 BCE, Roman armies intervened in southern Gaul to protect Massalia from local tribes. This led to the establishment of the Roman province of Gallia Transalpina, later known as Gallia Narbonensis (or simply "the Province"), which stretched from the Alps to the Pyrenees along the Mediterranean coast. Narbo Martius (modern Narbonne) became a key Roman settlement, serving as a hub for further expansion.

Roads and Infrastructure
The Romans were famous for their roads, and they quickly began building routes to connect Narbonensis with Italy and other regions. These roads allowed the swift movement of troops and goods. Over time, the convenience and security of Roman roads encouraged trade, boosted local economies, and led many Gallic tribes to see Rome not just as a threat but also as a source of stability and prosperity.

Diplomacy and Intervention
Rome's involvement in Gaul was not solely military. The Romans often used diplomacy and formed alliances, placing pro-Roman leaders in power among the tribes. However, tensions always remained. Some tribes resented Roman interference, while others tried to take advantage of alliances with Rome to dominate rival tribes. This complex web of alliances, hostilities, and shifting loyalties set the stage for larger conflicts.

The Gallic Wars

The single most crucial event that led to the Roman conquest of Gaul was the series of military campaigns known as the Gallic Wars, led by Julius Caesar from 58 BCE to 50 BCE. At the time, Caesar was a Roman general and politician looking to increase his power and prestige. Gaul offered him the perfect opportunity to win military glory.

Initial Reasons for Intervention
Caesar first entered Gaul under the pretext of defending Roman allies from attacks by migrating tribes like the Helvetii. Once there, he found reason after reason to campaign against various Gallic groups. His forces quickly defeated or subdued tribes that posed a challenge, often dividing them to prevent a united Gallic front.

Military Tactics and Roman Legions
Roman legions were disciplined, well-equipped, and experienced. Their training and engineering skills gave them an edge over most Gallic forces. Caesar also

excelled at siege warfare, constructing fortifications such as walls and towers with remarkable speed. During his campaigns, he built bridges and roads that allowed his legions to move quickly. He also knew how to employ diplomacy, setting certain tribes against one another.

Rebellion and Vercingetorix
Despite initial successes, the Gallic tribes grew increasingly resentful of Roman domination. The tipping point came around 52 BCE when a nobleman of the Arverni tribe, Vercingetorix, united many of the tribes against Caesar. Vercingetorix adopted a scorched-earth policy, destroying crops and towns so the Roman armies could not use them for supplies. The biggest showdown occurred at the Siege of Alesia, where Vercingetorix's forces were surrounded by Caesar's fortifications. A Gallic relief army tried to break through, but Roman engineering and organization prevailed. Ultimately, Vercingetorix surrendered, and the Gallic resistance collapsed.

Aftermath of the Conquest

With the defeat of Vercingetorix, most of Gaul fell under Roman control. Caesar's campaigns were brutal, resulting in a large loss of life and the enslavement of many Gauls. However, once subdued, many tribes were gradually integrated into Roman administration. The Romans collected taxes, stationed legions, built towns, and introduced Roman law and culture. Latin began to be used for official purposes, blending over time with local dialects.

Roman Administration
The Roman Empire reorganized Gaul into provinces, each overseen by a governor. These provinces had administrative capitals. Roads and aqueducts improved connectivity and sanitation. Romanization was stronger in urban centers, where temples, baths, forums, and theaters followed Roman architectural styles. In rural areas, many Gauls continued their traditional ways, though gradually adopting aspects of Roman life.

Cultural Changes
The Romans established their polytheistic religion alongside local Celtic deities. In some cases, Roman gods and Celtic gods were equated or merged. Over generations, this cultural blending gave rise to Gallo-Roman art, religion, and

identity. Elite Gauls might enter the Roman political system, learn Latin literature, and adopt Roman customs. The druidic religion lost power because the Romans discouraged it as a source of potential resistance.

Long-Term Significance
The Roman conquest laid the groundwork for the Roman province of Gaul, which would be crucial to the empire. Gaul became a prosperous territory, supplying grain, wine, metals, and soldiers to the Roman legions. Cities like Lugdunum (Lyon), Burdigala (Bordeaux), and Lutetia (Paris) grew from small settlements to major Roman towns. Roman law, language, infrastructure, and trade networks had a lasting impact, influencing the development of medieval and modern France.

Resistance and Accommodation

Not all Gauls accepted Roman rule peacefully. There were smaller revolts and localized resistance, but none matched the scale of Vercingetorix's uprising. Over time, as the Roman system brought stability, many Gauls found ways to benefit from it. They embraced trade opportunities, gained status by cooperating with Roman officials, and sent their children to Roman-style schools. This did not mean traditional culture vanished immediately. Many families held on to certain Celtic beliefs and practices, even as they engaged with the Roman world.

Gallic religion adapted, mixing Celtic gods with Roman ones. Some shrines combined practices from both traditions. The political environment also changed. Tribal chiefs who aligned with Rome became important intermediaries, helping to maintain order in the provinces. This balance between cooperation and cultural retention helped shape the region's identity.

Roman Gaul on the Eve of Empire

By the late 1st century BCE, Gaul was firmly in the hands of Rome. Julius Caesar's rise to power had profound effects on the Roman Republic, eventually leading to the end of the Republic and the beginning of the Empire under Augustus. Gaul was a major source of wealth and security for the new imperial system.

With roads linking towns, fortified camps protecting key points, and local elites supporting Roman governance, Gaul was now part of an international empire stretching across the Mediterranean. The shift from independent tribes to Roman provinces marked a historic transformation. The next steps in France's story would involve the gradual Romanization of the local population, the spread of Christianity, and, eventually, the fall of the Western Roman Empire.

Still, it is important to remember that this was not an overnight change. Tribal identities, Celtic traditions, and local ways of life persisted for centuries, merging with Roman customs to form a unique Gallo-Roman culture. The significance of the Gallic Wars and subsequent Roman conquest cannot be overstated: they reshaped the land's political structure, economy, culture, and language. This pivotal transition is the bridge between prehistoric tribal life and the more centralized world of classical antiquity.

In the next chapters, we will see how Roman Gaul developed under imperial rule, how Christianity took root, and how the forces that led to the eventual fall of Rome paved the way for new kingdoms and identities on the soil of what we now call France.

CHAPTER 3: ROMAN GAUL

Introduction

When the Gallic Wars ended and Julius Caesar defeated Vercingetorix, the land known as Gaul (covering most of present-day France and extending into surrounding regions) came firmly under Roman control. However, conquest was only the beginning of a long process. Over the next few centuries, Gaul would be reshaped by Roman administration, law, infrastructure, and culture. A new civilization, often called "Gallo-Roman," emerged as local Celtic traditions blended with Roman ways. This chapter will explore how Gaul was governed, how its economy and society changed, and how Christianity first took root in the region.

Roman Gaul did not form overnight. Various emperors played roles in organizing and reorganizing its provinces. New cities developed, Roman roads and aqueducts appeared, and a steady process of Romanization influenced daily life. Yet, many local customs persisted. Gauls adopted Roman dress, language, and architecture, but they often merged them with their own beliefs and art. Over time, Gallo-Roman culture became distinct in its own right.

One of the most significant developments in Roman Gaul was the spread of Christianity. Arriving at first in small groups, the new faith gradually grew, despite periods of persecution by Roman authorities. Eventually, Christianity became a major religious force. By the late empire, Gaul was not just a province; it was a key region, producing emperors and bishops who left their mark on European history.

Below, we will trace the administrative structure, economy, cultural life, and the early Christian communities in Gaul from the era of Augustus through the gradual transformations of the late Roman Empire.

1. The Formation of Roman Gaul Under Augustus

After Julius Caesar's victory, Rome had to consolidate its hold on Gaul. The civil wars that ended the Roman Republic also shaped the region. By the time Augustus (formerly Octavian) emerged as the first Roman emperor around 27 BCE, he began reorganizing the empire's territories for efficient governance and stability.

Reorganization and Administrative Changes

Augustus sought to strengthen the empire's borders. In Gaul, he refined provincial boundaries and improved tax collection. He also founded new settlements for veteran soldiers, creating loyalty among these communities. Gaul was split into various provinces, each governed by either a proconsul or a legate appointed by the emperor. This approach balanced local traditions with Roman oversight.

The Establishment of Lugdunum as a Major Center

One of Augustus's most notable projects in Gaul was the elevation of Lugdunum (present-day Lyon) to a major administrative and commercial hub. The city's central location, at the meeting of the Rhône and Saône Rivers, made it ideal for controlling trade routes. Augustus founded a new colony there, complete with Roman-style buildings, forums, and temples. Lugdunum became the seat of the imperial cult in Gaul, hosting yearly ceremonies in honor of the emperor and Rome.

Road Construction and Infrastructure

Roman power also rested on the ability to move troops and goods quickly. Augustus continued and expanded Caesar's legacy by building a network of roads. Some key routes linked southern Gaul to Italy, while others reached the Atlantic coast or northern territories. The roads served military, administrative, and economic needs. Legions could respond to unrest, tax collectors could travel effectively, and merchants could trade over long distances with less risk.

By the end of Augustus's reign, Gaul was no longer a patchwork of independent tribes. It was a set of Roman provinces, each with established cities, Roman-style governance, and increasing cultural exchange. Still, the local people did not vanish. They adapted to new structures, found roles in the Roman administration, and shaped the blend of traditions that would define Gallo-Roman identity.

---

2. The Provinces of Gaul

Over the first century CE, Roman officials refined Gaul's divisions. Different emperors made administrative changes, but broadly, Gaul fell into provinces like Gallia Narbonensis in the south, Gallia Aquitania in the southwest, Gallia Lugdunensis in the central region, and Gallia Belgica in the north. Later,

Diocletian's reforms in the late 3rd century would further subdivide these large provinces.

Gallia Narbonensis

Gallia Narbonensis stretched along the Mediterranean coast. Once called the Province (or "Provincia"), it was the oldest area of Roman control in Gaul, dating back to the second century BCE. The region held important ports, such as Massalia (Marseille) and Narbo Martius (Narbonne). With easy access to maritime trade routes, it quickly became prosperous. Vineyards, olive groves, and other Mediterranean-style agriculture thrived, tying the region's economy closely to that of Italy.

Gallia Aquitania

Southwestern Gaul, called Gallia Aquitania, included areas where Celtic and Aquitanian peoples lived. The Romans established several key settlements to control this region, benefiting from its agricultural output (especially grain and livestock). Over time, roads connected Aquitania to the rest of Gaul, making it an integral part of the empire's trade networks.

Gallia Lugdunensis

Named for its central city, Lugdunum, Gallia Lugdunensis covered much of central Gaul. It included the lands around the Loire Valley and extended up toward the Seine. Lugdunum itself was the administrative and religious heart, hosting the annual assembly of the Gauls where delegates from different provinces gathered. This meeting reinforced loyalty to Rome while allowing for regional coordination.

Gallia Belgica

In the north, Gallia Belgica bordered the Rhine frontier. This was a region of significant military interest because of the need to defend against Germanic tribes beyond the Rhine. Cities like Reims (Durocortorum) and Trier (Augusta Treverorum, though technically in present-day Germany) became crucial centers of Roman power. Later, as threats intensified, emperors would pay special attention to the fortifications along this frontier.

Through these provinces, Rome established both centralized oversight and a measure of local autonomy. Native elites often acted as mediators between their communities and Roman officials. In time, these elites embraced Roman citizenship, dressing like Romans, speaking Latin, and sending their sons to Roman schools.

3. The Gallo-Roman Economy

Gaul's economy under Rome was diverse and, for many centuries, vibrant. Agriculture formed the backbone of production. Wheat, barley, and other grains provided food surpluses, while wine and olive oil from the south were valuable exports. In other regions, livestock ranching, metal mining, and pottery manufacturing contributed to economic activity.

Agricultural Prosperity
Roman Gaul introduced or expanded farming techniques such as improved plow designs, crop rotation, and larger estates known as villae. Wealthy Gallo-Roman landowners lived in villa complexes, complete with mosaic floors and private baths. These villas were self-sufficient estates, producing not only grains and vegetables but also wine, olive oil (in southern areas), and raising animals.

Mining and Metalwork
Gaul had several metal resources, including iron, lead, and some silver deposits. Mining operations grew under Roman management, providing raw materials for weapons, tools, and currency. Smithing and metal craft became more refined, blending Celtic artistic traditions with Roman techniques. The region's metal production supported local economies and sometimes contributed to imperial needs, such as supplying the legions.

Trade Networks
Because Gaul lay between the Mediterranean and the northern seas, it served as a crossroad for goods moving throughout the empire. Ports in the south connected to Italy, Spain, and beyond. Rivers like the Rhône, Saône, and Loire carried ships inland. Roads extended commerce further, linking cities and smaller markets. Wine from Narbonensis might travel north, while ceramic goods from central Gaul or metals from the western parts could head south or east.

Urban Markets and Crafts
Cities grew into market centers. Artisans produced pottery, textiles, glassware, and other crafts. One famous example is Samian ware (terra sigillata), a high-quality red pottery often made in Gaul and traded widely across the empire. Skilled workers and merchants could gain wealth, and some became part of the city councils (curia). Over time, these city-based elites adopted Roman customs, reinforcing the empire's influence.

Despite periods of unrest, Gaul often prospered under Roman rule, especially in the first two centuries CE. Farms produced surpluses, trade routes were largely secure, and cities benefited from imperial investments in roads and public buildings. This prosperity helped lay the foundation for a lasting Gallo-Roman identity.

---

4. Gallo-Roman Society

Roman Gaul's society was a layered one, combining Roman social structures with older Celtic patterns. At the top were imperial officials and the wealthiest Gallo-Roman landowners. Below them, a varied middle group included city council members, merchants, and skilled artisans. The rural population—farmers, laborers, and slaves—formed the majority.

Local Elites and Roman Citizenship
Roman authorities realized that the easiest way to govern Gaul was by working with local elites. Over time, many of these elites received Roman citizenship. As citizens, they could hold public office in Roman administration, join the legions as officers, or even climb the imperial ranks. In the process, they started wearing togas, speaking Latin, and building homes in the Roman style. Some wealthy Gauls even traveled to Rome, seeking influence at the imperial court.

Slaves and Freedmen
Slavery was a part of Roman society. In Gaul, slaves could come from war captives, debtors, or the offspring of existing slaves. They worked on farms, in mines, or as household servants. However, the Roman system also allowed for manumission—the freeing of slaves. Freed slaves became freedmen, a social class with fewer privileges than free-born citizens but still able to hold property and pass on wealth to their children. Over generations, some freedmen's families integrated into mainstream Gallo-Roman society.

Cultural Blending
As Roman and Gaulish cultures merged, everyday life showed signs of both. People might worship Roman gods like Jupiter or Mars in temples but still honor local deities at rural shrines. The Latin language spread, especially in towns and administrative centers, but local dialects survived in many rural areas for a long time. Gallo-Roman art often used Roman forms (like mosaics, statues, and reliefs) but included Celtic patterns or themes.

Education and Literacy
The Roman presence brought formal schooling to Gaul's cities. Children of the elite studied grammar, rhetoric, and literature, mostly in Latin. Some also learned Greek, considered the language of higher learning in the Roman world. While general literacy levels are hard to measure, inscriptions and documents show that at least the upper and middle classes embraced reading and writing in Latin, helping tie them closer to Roman administrative and cultural life.

---

5. Urban Life in Roman Gaul

Cities in Roman Gaul served as centers of governance, commerce, and culture. Each city typically featured certain standard Roman buildings and structures: a forum, baths, temples, amphitheaters, and sometimes theaters or circuses (for chariot races). These public spaces became gathering points for festivals and daily socializing.

Public Buildings and Amenities
Roman baths were especially popular. They were not just places to wash but also centers of leisure, exercise, and conversation. Cities with large bath complexes, such as those found in Lugdunum or Trier, displayed the wealth and sophistication of local elites. Aqueducts supplied fresh water, and sewer systems carried waste away, improving public health and comfort.

Entertainment and Leisure
Amphitheaters hosted gladiatorial games, animal hunts, and public spectacles. Although gladiators were often slaves or condemned criminals, the games drew huge crowds. Some cities also had theaters where plays, musical performances, or recitations took place. These events allowed the local population—both Roman and Gaulish—to see Roman-style entertainment up close.

Religious Life
Temples honored Roman gods, the imperial cult, and sometimes local deities. People made offerings, held processions, and marked important days on the religious calendar. The emperors' birthdays and major Roman festivals were celebrated with sacrifices, banquets, and games. Through these rituals, city dwellers participated in a shared Roman identity, even if they retained older Celtic or regional customs in private.

Urban Planning and Defense

Many cities in Gaul were laid out with a grid pattern, inspired by Roman urban design. Streets intersected at right angles, and central forums contained administrative buildings. In areas threatened by raids, defensive walls were built. Over time, especially in the later empire, cities began fortifying themselves as external pressures grew. Urban life remained vibrant, but the cost of defense rose, and the shape of the cities changed to adapt to the new realities.

---

6. The Emergence of Gallo-Roman Culture

While Rome imposed its language and administrative framework, Gaul had deep Celtic roots that did not vanish. Instead, a distinct Gallo-Roman culture developed. Archaeological finds—like jewelry that blends Celtic motifs with Roman techniques—show the artistic fusion. Inscriptions on altars sometimes invoke both Roman gods and Celtic gods, reflecting a religious blending as well.

Language and Literature

Latin became the dominant language of administration and trade. Over the centuries, Vulgar Latin (the spoken form of Latin) in Gaul began to take on local characteristics, influenced by the speech habits of native Celtic speakers. This evolving form of Latin would eventually become the ancestor of the French language. While classical Latin was used for inscriptions and official texts, everyday speech slowly diverged from the standard taught in schools.

Art and Architecture

Mosaic floors with geometric or mythological scenes adorned wealthy villas. Statues and reliefs might show Roman gods but with local styles of carving. In some places, the Celtic tradition of large stone sculptures of heads blended with Roman portraiture styles. Public buildings often followed Roman models, yet local stones and styles of decoration added regional flavors.

Religious Syncretism

Many Celtic deities found parallels among Roman gods. For example, the Celtic god Lugus was sometimes associated with Mercury. Shrines and temples might combine architecture from both traditions. This syncretism made the new religion more acceptable to local populations. Even the druids, once powerful in Celtic society, gradually faded from prominence, although some aspects of their spiritual practices found smaller forms of continuity in local folk beliefs.

Local Identity and Pride
Though they were part of the Roman Empire, many Gallo-Romans maintained a sense of their own heritage. They celebrated local festivals, told stories of tribal ancestors, and honored the memory of heroic figures from their Celtic past. Over time, being Gallo-Roman meant belonging to both a Roman political world and a local cultural one. This dual identity helped keep the region stable for long periods, as people had reasons to be loyal to Rome but also to preserve unique traditions.

---

7. Military and Frontier Defense

Gaul was vital to Rome's frontier strategy, especially along the Rhine River. By the 1st century CE, the empire had established military camps and fortresses to monitor and repel Germanic incursions. Soldiers stationed in these border zones influenced local life, bringing new demands for supplies and creating opportunities for merchants. Towns often sprang up around forts, providing services to the soldiers.

Legions and Auxiliaries
Roman legions stationed in Gaul recruited men from the local population, offering pay, land, and citizenship upon completion of service. Auxilia (auxiliary forces) included cavalry and specialized troops from various parts of the empire. Over time, many Gauls rose in the ranks to become centurions or even higher officers. This military involvement further strengthened ties between Gaul and the imperial center.

Fortifications and Watchtowers
Along the Rhine, and later along other vulnerable borders, the Romans built walls, watchtowers, and small forts. Roads connected these forts so that troops could move quickly if enemy tribes attacked. The presence of the army also shaped the economy, as local farmers sold grain and livestock to supply the troops.

Raids and Regional Instability
Despite these defenses, Gaul faced periodic raids by Germanic groups. Most of these attacks were small-scale, aiming for plunder. However, larger invasions occasionally threatened the provinces. When Roman power was strong, these invasions were repelled. But during times of internal strife or weak imperial leadership, the frontiers became more vulnerable.

The balance between a strong military presence and local autonomy allowed Gaul to enjoy relative peace for much of the early imperial period. Yet, by the 3rd century, crises within the empire would make this balance harder to maintain.

---

8. The Crisis of the 3rd Century and the "Gallic Empire"

From around 235 to 284 CE, the Roman Empire faced a series of internal and external crises often called the "Crisis of the Third Century." Emperors rose and fell rapidly, barbarian groups took advantage of the turmoil to press on borders, and economic troubles, including inflation, rocked the provinces. Gaul was not spared from these challenges.

Invasions and Internal Strife
Germanic tribes such as the Alamanni and Franks (not yet the dominant group they would become later) made repeated incursions into Gaul. At the same time, Roman armies were busy fighting on multiple fronts, and emperors struggled to hold the empire together. Local leaders in Gaul worried that the central government could no longer protect them effectively.

The Breakaway Gallic Empire
In 260 CE, a Roman general named Postumus set up an independent state in Gaul, sometimes called the "Gallic Empire." This entity included Gaul, parts of Germany, and even Britain. Postumus declared himself emperor, claiming he could defend these territories better than the emperor in Rome. He established a capital at Cologne (in modern Germany) and minted his own coins.

For a while, this Gallic Empire offered stability in the region. Postumus successfully repelled invasions, gaining support from local elites who welcomed strong leadership. However, this state did not last long. Postumus was killed by his own troops in 269 CE, and internal struggles weakened his successors. Eventually, Emperor Aurelian reunited the breakaway provinces with the Roman Empire in 274 CE.

Significance of the Gallic Empire
Although brief, the Gallic Empire showed that Gaul had developed a sense of its own identity and resources. The event highlighted the empire-wide fractures of the 3rd century and foreshadowed future divisions. Even after the region was brought back under central Roman rule, the seeds of local autonomy remained.

These seeds would matter greatly when Rome's power declined again in later centuries.

9. The Spread of Early Christianity in Gaul

While Gaul was dealing with military crises, a new religious movement was taking root across the empire: Christianity. It likely reached Gaul through merchants, travelers, and soldiers who had encountered it elsewhere. By the 2nd and 3rd centuries, small Christian communities had formed in cities like Lugdunum, Vienne, and elsewhere.

Early Christian Communities
The earliest Christians in Gaul were a minority, often meeting in private homes or discreet gatherings. They included people from various social backgrounds—some were slaves, others were traders, and a few were educated elites seeking spiritual fulfillment beyond the Roman gods. Because the Roman state saw Christians as a suspicious group that refused to worship the emperor or make sacrifices to Roman deities, Christians sometimes faced hostility.

Persecution
One notable incident was the persecution of Christians in Lugdunum in 177 CE during the reign of Emperor Marcus Aurelius. Early Christian leaders like St. Irenaeus wrote letters and treatises defending their faith. Although persecution flared up at different times, Christianity survived and slowly grew. By the early 4th century, Emperor Constantine's conversion and the Edict of Milan (313 CE) offered Christians imperial protection, leading to more rapid expansion.

Bishops and Church Organization
As Christianity became more accepted, bishops emerged as important local leaders. They oversaw religious matters, organized charity, and sometimes acted as mediators with Roman authorities. In Gaul, prominent bishops like Martin of Tours (4th century) became famous for their missionary work and for helping spread Christian beliefs beyond urban centers into rural areas. Churches and monasteries began to appear, providing social and spiritual services.

Transformation of Religious Life
The acceptance of Christianity changed the religious landscape of Gaul. Pagan temples lost some of their influence as churches gained prominence. Over time,

many older shrines were abandoned or repurposed. Still, elements of traditional Celtic and Roman beliefs lingered among the population, merging in some cases with Christian practices. But by the late 4th and early 5th centuries, Christianity had established a strong foundation in Gaul, influencing moral teachings, social norms, and local governance.

---

10. The Dominate Period and Tensions in the Late Empire

By the late 3rd and early 4th century, the Roman government underwent reforms under Emperors Diocletian and Constantine. This period is often called the Dominate, marking a shift from the earlier Principate. Emperors now claimed more absolute power, wore elaborate court dress, and were distanced from ordinary citizens. Diocletian divided the empire into multiple administrative zones, each ruled by an emperor or caesar, hoping to manage crises more effectively.

Administrative Overhauls in Gaul
In Gaul, this meant more provinces and smaller administrative units, all grouped into a larger "diocese" under a vicarius. The capital sometimes shifted to cities like Treverorum (Trier) for better oversight of the Rhine frontier. Army reforms tried to create mobile forces that could respond quickly to invasions. These measures did bring some stability, but they also led to heavier taxation to support a larger bureaucracy and standing army.

Economic and Social Pressures
Heavy taxes and mandatory service obligations weighed on farmers and landowners. Over time, some free farmers fell into debt and became tenant farmers on large estates. Rural villas fortified themselves against raids, while city walls became ever more important. The once-thriving trade networks faced disruptions from constant warfare and internal disputes. The empire still functioned, but the strain was visible.

Increasing Barbarian Pressures
Germanic peoples across the Rhine were becoming more organized. Groups like the Franks, Alamanni, and Vandals grew in strength. While Rome could still negotiate treaties or hold them off in some cases, breaches in defenses happened more often. The 4th century also saw the Huns moving westward, pushing other

tribes in front of them. This chain reaction would eventually spill into Gaul with devastating impact.

Religious Unity and Division

Even as the empire tried to unify around Christianity, theological disputes and heresies sometimes caused internal rifts. Councils were held, bishops argued over doctrine, and emperors intervened in church affairs. In Gaul, most church leaders supported the decisions of major councils like Nicaea (325 CE), reinforcing a certain unity. However, sects and rivalries still popped up, especially in times of social stress.

By the end of the 4th century, Gaul was a mix of Roman traditions, Christian faith, and lingering Celtic customs. The empire was centralized in theory, but local power structures—like bishops and large landowners—began filling gaps. The stage was set for a final series of upheavals that would break Roman authority in the west.

Conclusion

During the period of Roman rule, Gaul evolved from a cluster of tribes to a network of Roman provinces, each with its own cities, roads, and administrative systems. A distinct Gallo-Roman culture developed, preserving Celtic elements within a Roman framework. Economic prosperity in the early centuries gave way to crises in the 3rd century, culminating in temporary breakaway states like the "Gallic Empire." Although reunited under Rome, Gaul remained a crucial region where threats from across the Rhine were always near.

Christianity introduced a new layer of identity for many people in Gaul. Initially persecuted, it eventually gained the empire's support and transformed religious practices and community life. By the 4th and early 5th centuries, the church held growing influence. Bishops played both spiritual and social roles, mediating between local communities and imperial powers.

Despite reforms, the Roman Empire became more strained. Barbarian pressures mounted, and heavy taxation plus military demands eroded loyalty and stability. Gaul, once the prosperous pride of the empire, would soon face waves of invaders and a dramatic shift in power. The next chapter will explore how the Western Roman Empire fell apart in Gaul and how new forces, most notably the Franks, set the stage for the medieval period.

CHAPTER 4: THE FALL OF ROME AND THE RISE OF THE FRANKS

Introduction

By the turn of the 5th century, the Roman Empire in the West was on the brink of collapse. Repeated attacks by Germanic and other "barbarian" groups, combined with internal weaknesses, left frontier defenses in tatters. Gaul, a key province for trade and troop movements, became a major battleground. Various tribes—Visigoths, Vandals, Burgundians, and others—moved into or across Gaul in search of new lands. In this chaos, the Franks began to emerge as a dominant force.

This chapter examines the downfall of Roman authority in Gaul and how the Franks took advantage of the situation. We will see how local Roman leaders, bishops, and military commanders tried to hold things together, but ultimately, new kingdoms formed. As Roman power faded, different tribal groups carved out their own territories. Among these, the Franks eventually gained a decisive edge under leaders like Clovis, setting in motion the foundations of what would become medieval France.

1. The Barbarian Invasions

During the 4th century, pressures along Rome's frontiers grew. The Huns' westward advance forced other tribes to flee or migrate, causing a domino effect. In 406 CE, a massive group of Vandals, Alans, and Suebi crossed the frozen Rhine into Gaul. This event is often seen as a critical blow to the Western Empire's ability to control the region.

Vandal and Alan Movements
The Vandals, a Germanic people, along with the Iranian Alans, swept through Gaul. They plundered cities and rural estates, causing widespread destruction. Many Gallo-Roman landowners fled to safer regions or fortified their villas. Some made deals with the invaders to protect their lands, but overall, the Roman administration failed to mount an effective defense.

Visigoths Enter Gaul

The Visigoths, under King Alaric, had already sacked Rome in 410 CE, shocking the empire. They eventually moved into southern Gaul and northern Spain. The Roman government, desperate for stability, struck a deal with them. The Visigoths settled in Aquitania (around Toulouse) as "foederati," meaning they were granted lands in exchange for military service. This arrangement provided temporary relief but further fragmented Roman control.

Burgundians in Eastern Gaul

Another Germanic group, the Burgundians, also found a foothold in Gaul. They settled around the Rhine and later moved into regions near the Alps and the Rhône Valley. They established a kingdom with Lyon as an important center. Like the Visigoths, the Burgundians came in initially as allies of Rome, but they soon acted with significant independence.

---

2. Roman Authority Weakens

As these various groups carved out territories in Gaul, Roman power became more symbolic than real. The emperors in Ravenna (the Western capital after Rome) or their local representatives could do little to reverse the tide. A few Gallo-Roman aristocrats tried to preserve order, but their resources were limited.

Local Defense by Roman Generals

Some Roman generals in Gaul, such as Aetius, played crucial roles in defending the region. Aetius, known as the "last of the Romans," formed alliances with different groups, including the Huns, to battle other invaders. He famously defeated Attila the Hun at the Battle of the Catalaunian Plains (451 CE) near Châlons-en-Champagne. While this victory was significant, it did not stop the overall decline of Roman influence in Gaul.

Rise of Regional Powers

With the Roman central government nearly powerless, local military commanders, bishops, and noble families became the real authorities. Cities often had to fend for themselves, raising militias or negotiating with nearby tribes. Some Gallo-Roman leaders cooperated with invaders if it meant security for their people. Others resisted, hoping for a resurgence of Roman might that never truly came.

Bishops as Civic Leaders
In many cities, bishops took on civic duties. They organized the distribution of food, negotiated truces, and oversaw the rebuilding of walls. Figures like Bishop Germanus of Auxerre or Bishop Eucherius of Lyon became moral and practical leaders, stepping into roles once filled by Roman magistrates. The church's growing influence shaped the transition from Roman to post-Roman Gaul.

---

3. The Franks

Among the various groups pushing into Gaul, the Franks stand out. Originally from regions east of the Rhine, the Franks were divided into different sub-groups, such as the Salians and the Ripuarians. They first entered Roman Gaul as foederati, similar to the Visigoths, meaning they settled in frontier areas in exchange for military service.

Early Frankish Leaders
By the late 4th and early 5th centuries, Frankish chieftains had established small enclaves within Gaul, mainly in the north (around the lower Rhine). They were known for their formidable warriors and flexible alliances. Roman generals often hired Frankish troops to bolster defenses against other raiders. In this way, certain Frankish leaders gained recognition and even minor Roman titles.

Clovis's Father: Childeric I
One key figure in this transitional period was Childeric I, a Frankish leader who held power around Tournai. He served as a Roman military commander in northern Gaul. When the Roman administration weakened, Childeric continued to expand his influence, often allying with local Gallo-Roman officials who preferred the Franks over rival invaders. This laid the groundwork for his son, Clovis, to build a larger kingdom.

Frankish Identity and Warfare
The Franks had a strong warrior culture. Their war bands prized loyalty to a chief and success in battle. They also displayed a certain adaptability. Unlike some tribes, they did not quickly move on to distant parts of the empire. Instead, they settled in northern Gaul, intermarried with local populations, and built lasting power bases. This approach gave them an advantage over groups that passed through Gaul on their way to Spain or Africa.

4. Collapse of the Western Empire

By the mid-5th century, the Western Roman Empire was in disarray. Emperors were frequently figureheads, placed on the throne by powerful generals or Germanic kings. The position of "Emperor of the West" effectively ended in 476 CE when the Germanic commander Odoacer deposed the last emperor, Romulus Augustulus, in Italy. While this date is often given as the "fall" of the Western Empire, in Gaul the process had been underway for decades.

Power Vacuums in Gaul
With no effective imperial authority, local powers in Gaul either declared independence or pledged allegiance to nearby barbarian kings. The Visigoths held much of southwestern Gaul, the Burgundians controlled the southeast, and smaller groups occupied pockets elsewhere. The Franks were consolidating power in the north. Some Gallo-Roman leaders, like Syagrius in the region around Soissons, tried to keep a remnant of Roman rule alive, but they stood alone.

Roman Institutions in Decline
Traditional Roman institutions—courts, city councils, and tax systems—withered or adapted to new rulers. Many administrative officials either fled or shifted allegiance to whichever king promised stability. Latin remained a language of the church and the educated classes, but the day-to-day governance now rested with whoever held military might.

Cultural Continuity
Despite the political collapse, much of Roman culture did not disappear overnight. Many aristocratic families in Gaul continued to practice a Roman lifestyle, at least privately. They maintained villas, read classical texts, and wore Roman dress. The church also preserved Latin literacy. Over time, however, these Roman patterns mixed further with Germanic customs, laying the groundwork for medieval society.

---

5. The Rise of Clovis and the Frankish Kingdom

The most pivotal figure in the transition from Roman Gaul to medieval Francia was Clovis, son of Childeric I. Born around 466 CE, Clovis became king of the Salian Franks in the 480s. He quickly set about expanding his realm, using both diplomacy and force.

Victory over Syagrius (486 CE)
Clovis's first major move was to confront Syagrius, the last Gallo-Roman ruler in northern Gaul. In 486 CE, Clovis defeated Syagrius's forces near Soissons. This victory ended Roman-style governance in the region and gave the Franks control over a significant part of northern Gaul. The battle boosted Clovis's reputation and attracted more warriors to his banner.

Expansion into Other Regions
After securing the north, Clovis turned his attention to rival Frankish chiefs and neighboring Germanic groups. He managed to subdue some by force, while in other cases he used alliances and marriages to unify the Franks under his leadership. This consolidation allowed him to present a more formidable front against the Burgundians and Visigoths.

Conversion to Christianity
One of the most defining moments in Clovis's rise was his conversion to Nicene Christianity (as opposed to the Arian Christianity followed by some other Germanic kings). The exact date is traditionally placed around 496 CE, often linked to his victory over the Alamanni. According to later accounts, Clovis promised to convert if he won the battle. After his baptism, he gained the crucial support of Gallo-Roman bishops and Christian communities, who were relieved to see a powerful barbarian king embrace their faith.

Political Implications of Conversion
By choosing Nicene Christianity, Clovis aligned himself with the majority of church leaders in Gaul. This gave him legitimacy in the eyes of the local Roman population and the bishops, who became important allies in administration. Many aristocrats, still strongly Christian, welcomed Clovis's rule over that of Arian Visigoths or Burgundians. This acceptance smoothed his expansion throughout Gaul.

---

6. Conflict with the Visigoths and Burgundians

With his northern power secure, Clovis looked to the south. The Visigoths under King Alaric II held much of Aquitania, including the wealthy city of Toulouse. The Burgundians, led by King Gundobad, controlled areas around the Rhône. Clovis's ambition to rule all of Gaul set him on a collision course with these neighbors.

War Against the Visigoths
A major conflict erupted in 507 CE. Clovis marched against Alaric II, claiming to protect Nicene Christians in Visigothic territory, where the ruling class was Arian. The decisive battle took place at Vouillé (near Poitiers), resulting in a Frankish victory and the death of Alaric II. Clovis gained a large part of southwestern Gaul, forcing the Visigoths to retreat to Septimania (a narrow coastal strip around Narbonne).

Dealings with the Burgundians
Clovis did not fully conquer the Burgundian kingdom, but he exerted pressure and used political marriages to expand his influence. Later Frankish kings would continue these efforts, eventually subjugating the Burgundians. For now, Clovis established himself as the most powerful ruler in Gaul, overshadowing the Burgundians, the remaining Visigoths, and other smaller kingdoms.

---

7. The Formation of a Frankish Realm

By the time of his death in 511 CE, Clovis had laid the foundations of a unified Frankish kingdom covering a large portion of Gaul. This new realm combined Frankish and Gallo-Roman elements in government, law, and culture. Bishops served as administrators and advisors, while Frankish chiefs continued to command armies.

Merovingian Dynasty
Clovis's family line is known as the Merovingians. After his death, his kingdom was divided among his sons, following Frankish custom. Though this often led to internal conflicts, the Merovingian dynasty still held onto most of Gaul. The strong identification with Nicene Christianity kept the support of local church leaders.

The Lex Salica
To administer law, the Franks used a mix of Roman traditions and their own customs. One notable code was the Lex Salica, a set of Frankish legal rules that addressed crimes, inheritance, and property. While it did not completely replace Roman law—especially in cities with large Gallo-Roman populations—it served as a foundation for how the Franks settled disputes. Over time, Gallo-Roman law and Frankish law influenced each other, reflecting the blending of cultures.

Cultural Transformation

Under Frankish rule, Latin remained an important language of the church and administration, but the Frankish language also spread among the elite. Art and architecture began to shift, with fewer monumental Roman buildings constructed and more emphasis on wooden structures or simpler stone churches. The older Roman cities adapted to new political realities, often shrinking in size, while rural estates (some still occupied by Roman aristocrats) became central to local economies.

---

8. The Church's Role in the New Kingdom

The church played a central role in the formation of the Frankish kingdom. Since Clovis's baptism, bishops had supported his regime as a protector of Nicene Christianity. Monasteries spread, founded by devout Christians who wanted to live apart from worldly affairs. Monks and nuns provided charity, preserved texts, and maintained religious traditions.

Bishops as Power Brokers

Because they were literate and had organizational skills, bishops served as counselors to Frankish kings. They helped manage taxes, record laws, and oversee education (such as it existed) for the aristocracy. Bishoprics in major cities like Reims, Tours, and Paris became centers of both religious and political power. The bishop of Rome (the pope) also began to play an increasing role in Western politics, though communication with Gaul was not always easy.

Monastic Communities

Figures like St. Martin of Tours (who lived earlier, in the 4th century) had inspired monasticism in Gaul. By the 6th century, monasteries were scattered throughout the countryside. They followed various rules, providing spiritual retreats and sometimes acting as schools for young nobles. These communities helped preserve the remnants of Roman learning, including Latin texts and histories.

Christianization of the Countryside

While cities had embraced Christianity earlier, rural areas often clung to old pagan practices. Missionaries, supported by bishops or noble patrons, traveled to villages and built small chapels. Over generations, pagan shrines and sacred groves were replaced by Christian churches or adapted to Christian worship. By the end of the 6th century, the majority of Gaul's population identified as Christian in some form, although many local customs persisted under a Christian veneer.

9. Challenges After Clovis

Though Clovis had united much of Gaul, his death led to a division of his realm among his sons—Theuderic, Chlodomer, Childebert, and Clothar. Each son ruled a portion, centering on different key cities like Reims, Orléans, Paris, and Soissons. These divisions sparked power struggles, as each branch of the Merovingian family tried to expand at the others' expense.

Civil Wars and Alliances
Over the 6th century, Frankish Gaul saw frequent civil wars. Alliances shifted, and noble families vied for influence at each royal court. Sometimes bishops intervened to prevent or mitigate conflict, but they could not stop the underlying competition. These internal disputes slowed down any chance of strong centralized authority.

Continued Conflicts with Neighboring Kingdoms
The Merovingian rulers also continued to face external threats. The Burgundian kingdom, though partially integrated, still maintained some independence until it was fully conquered. The Visigoths remained entrenched in Septimania. Meanwhile, to the east, other Germanic groups watched for opportunities to gain territory.

Long-Term Effects
Even with these internal challenges, the Frankish dominance of Gaul stood firm. Over time, the various branches of the Merovingian family reunited parts of the kingdom through marriage or conquest. The idea that Gaul was a Frankish land took root, shaping the region's identity and distinguishing it from the older Roman Empire.

---

10. The Transition to Medieval France

By the end of the 6th century, the transformation of Gaul from a Roman province into a patchwork of Frankish kingdoms was largely complete. Roman political structures had faded away. What remained was a hybrid system: kings with Germanic heritage ruling over a mostly Romanized population in close partnership with the Christian church.

Decline of Roman Urban Life
Roman cities had once been vibrant centers of trade and administration. Under the

Franks, urban life changed. Some cities fell into disrepair, losing population as security threats and shifting economies pushed people to the countryside. Others adapted, retaining their walls and forming smaller cores around cathedrals and bishop's palaces. This urban decline was a key feature of the early Middle Ages, although not every city collapsed. Lyon and other major centers remained important, albeit on a reduced scale.

Shift in Aristocratic Power
With the fall of Rome, many large landowners became de facto local rulers. The Merovingian kings depended on them for armies and administration. In return, these landowners gained privileges and partial autonomy. Over time, this relationship laid the groundwork for feudalism. But in the 5th and 6th centuries, it was still in its early stages. The main unifying factors were the king, the church, and a shared Christian identity that transcended some local divisions.

Language and Culture
Latin remained the administrative and liturgical language. Yet, the spoken Latin in Gaul was evolving into various local dialects, which would eventually become Old French and other regional tongues. Frankish words entered the local speech, especially in military or agricultural contexts. Artistic expressions, too, showed a blend: Roman techniques fused with Germanic designs, leading to new forms in jewelry, sculpture, and manuscript illumination.

Seeds of the Medieval Period
By 600 CE, Gaul was firmly in the hands of the Merovingian Franks. The Western Roman Empire was a memory. A new political and cultural landscape emerged: kingdoms ruled by warrior-kings, local lords, and bishops, bound together by Christian faith and shared interests. Trade continued on a smaller scale, and literacy survived primarily in church settings. These conditions would shape the Middle Ages, as future chapters will explore how the Merovingians evolved and eventually gave way to the Carolingians and beyond.

CHAPTER 5: THE MEROVINGIANS AND THE SHAPING OF EARLY MEDIEVAL FRANCE

Introduction

When Clovis died in 511 CE, he left behind a sizable kingdom in Gaul, ruled by the Frankish Merovingian dynasty. But his death also led to a division of territory among his sons, as was customary among the Franks. Despite periodic civil wars, internal power struggles, and shifting alliances, the Merovingian line endured for over two centuries. During this time, the foundations of medieval France began to take shape.

In this chapter, we will examine how the Merovingians governed, how their internal conflicts both splintered and reshaped the kingdom, and how the partnership between the Frankish kings and the church evolved. We will also explore the roles of prominent queens, noble families, and local officials. All these factors influenced the political landscape, social structures, and cultural life of early medieval France.

By the middle of the 8th century, the Merovingian kings still held the throne in name, but real power often lay in the hands of the "Mayors of the Palace." These influential officials set the stage for a major transition: the rise of the Carolingian dynasty. Understanding Merovingian rule is essential for grasping the roots of medieval French governance, law, and identity.

1. The Division of Clovis's Kingdom

Clovis left four sons: Theuderic, Chlodomer, Childebert, and Clothar. According to Frankish tradition, a kingdom was considered the personal possession of the king. So when a king died, his lands were divided among his male heirs. This principle shaped Merovingian politics and often led to conflicts among royal siblings.

Four Kingdoms

After Clovis's death, Gaul was split into four sub-kingdoms, each with its own capital:

- Theuderic reigned in Metz (in the northeastern region).
- Chlodomer held Orléans (central Gaul).
- Childebert ruled from Paris (north-central).
- Clothar governed from Soissons (north).

Initially, these kingdoms were merely subdivisions, but competition soon turned them into separate political arenas. Each brother sought to expand his realm at the expense of the others. Alliances formed and broke apart, sometimes leading to open war.

Impact on Administration

Despite divisions, the brothers and their successors recognized a shared Frankish identity and a continuing partnership with the Gallic church. Bishops often acted as mediators, trying to maintain some unity. Still, the frequent reshuffling of territories complicated local governance. Officials in border regions had to switch loyalties if their region was transferred from one Merovingian brother to another.

Continuing the Legacy of Clovis

Clovis's most enduring achievement was the partnership with the Nicene (Catholic) Church. Even in the midst of sibling rivalry, the sons generally kept favorable ties with bishops and clergy, ensuring that Christianity remained a unifying force. The memory of Clovis's conversion was invoked to legitimize new kings. If a ruler acted too harshly against the church, he risked losing moral and political support.

---

2. Rival Merovingian Kingdoms

Over the course of the 6th and 7th centuries, Merovingian lands gradually coalesced into three main sub-kingdoms: Austrasia in the east (around Metz), Neustria in the northwest (around Soissons and Paris), and Burgundy in the southeast (centered near Lyon and Geneva). These divisions changed over time, but they became recognizable entities within the broader Frankish realm.

Austrasia

Austrasia roughly encompassed the Rhine frontier, eastern Gaul, and parts of modern-day Germany. This region often faced border pressures from Germanic tribes and had a strong warrior tradition. The eastern position encouraged a focus on defense and expansion toward the Rhine and beyond. Important cities included Metz and Reims.

Neustria
Neustria formed the western and northern heartland of the Frankish territories, including areas around Paris, Soissons, and the lower Seine. This region was often considered the old core of Clovis's power. Neustria tended to be wealthier and more Romanized, with cities that had been central in late Roman Gaul.

Burgundy
Originally the territory of the Burgundians, this region was conquered and incorporated into the Frankish kingdom. Over time, it became its own sub-kingdom under various Merovingian rulers. Burgundy included the Rhône Valley and parts of the Alps region. It had strong Gallo-Roman influences, a distinct local culture, and strategic trade routes leading to the Mediterranean.

Shifting Borders and Alliances
Merovingian kings and princes frequently contested control of these regions. Marriages, assassinations, and treaties rearranged borders. Sometimes, a ruler gained control over two or even all three sub-kingdoms, forming a brief unity. However, succession rules typically unraveled such unification upon the king's death. This constant flux defined Merovingian politics.

---

3. The Role of Royal Women and Noble Families

In Merovingian Gaul, royal women—queens, princesses, and noblewomen—sometimes wielded great influence. They served as regents for underage kings, arranged marriages that sealed political alliances, and patronized churches and monasteries. At times, their actions decisively shaped the balance of power within the dynasty.

Queen Clotilde
One early example is Queen Clotilde, the wife of Clovis. Although her major influence was in encouraging Clovis's conversion, her role extended beyond that event. After Clovis's death, she attempted to mediate among her sons. Later, she

withdrew to a life of piety and became revered as a saint, reflecting the intertwining of royalty and religious devotion in Merovingian society.

Brunhilda and Fredegunda

Two of the most famous (or infamous) royal women were Brunhilda (a Visigothic princess married into the Austrasian line) and Fredegunda (a Neustrian queen consort). Their rivalry in the late 6th and early 7th centuries ignited civil wars that ravaged the Frankish realm.

- **Brunhilda** governed Austrasia as a regent for her sons and grandsons. She tried to centralize the administration, supporting loyal bishops and nobles to counteract rebellious magnates. Her strong hand made her many enemies at court.
- **Fredegunda**, wife of King Chilperic I, was known for political cunning and ruthless actions. She orchestrated assassinations and forged alliances to eliminate rivals.

Their feud became legendary, fueling a long period of warfare between Austrasia and Neustria-Burgundy. Eventually, Brunhilda fell from power, captured by King Clothar II (Fredegunda's son), who executed her in a brutal manner. This ended one of the most turbulent chapters of Merovingian politics.

Noble Families

Beyond the royal family, powerful aristocratic lineages emerged. They controlled large estates, held military commands, and served as regional governors or counts. As the Merovingians struggled among themselves, these noble families played kingmakers, throwing their support behind different heirs. In return, they expected grants of land, titles, and exemptions. Over time, some of these families gained nearly autonomous power in their respective regions.

---

4. The Church's Growing Influence

The partnership between Merovingian kings and the church continued to deepen. Bishops, monks, and nuns not only shaped religious life but also became essential in governance, land administration, and cultural preservation. Monasteries sprang up across Gaul, supported by donations from both kings and nobles.

Monastic Foundations

Many Merovingian rulers and noble families founded monasteries as expressions of piety and as a means to exert regional influence. Monastic communities often received tax exemptions, land grants, and other privileges. In exchange, the monks or nuns prayed for the founders' souls, provided education to local youths, and sometimes offered charitable services.

Bishops as Administrators

In major cities, bishops took on increasing civic responsibilities. They acted as mediators between local populations and the king's court, managing disputes and organizing defense when needed. Over time, some bishops came from or were closely allied with powerful noble families, further linking the church hierarchy to secular power structures.

Synods and Councils

During the Merovingian era, church synods and councils became more common. These gatherings brought together bishops from various regions to discuss doctrinal issues, discipline within the clergy, and the moral obligations of Christian rulers. While these councils did not override the king's authority, they did help establish church standards and canons that both secular and religious leaders were expected to respect.

Missionary Work

Although Gaul was largely Christian by this time, certain rural areas still preserved pagan customs. Monks and missionary bishops expanded Christian practices into the countryside. Over time, popular festivals and sacred sites were adapted to Christian rites, blending Celtic, Roman, and Frankish traditions into a localized Christian culture.

---

5. Law and Order

Under the Merovingians, law was a blend of Roman legal ideas and Germanic customs. Clovis's successors continued to use the Lex Salica for the Franks, but also allowed Gallo-Romans to follow modified forms of Roman law. This dual system slowly evolved into a patchwork of legal traditions.

Salic Law and Its Influence

Salic Law (Lex Salica) dealt with a variety of matters: theft, murder, inheritance, and property disputes. It established a system of wergild—monetary compensation for injuries or deaths—rather than relying purely on vengeance. This approach sought to reduce blood feuds among the Franks. Over time, adjustments were made, and other tribal laws (like Ripuarian Law) also appeared.

Roman Law Continuity
In regions more heavily influenced by Roman administration, local communities still remembered Roman legal procedures, especially regarding contracts, property rights, and civic obligations. Bishops and local judges sometimes referenced both Roman precedents and Germanic custom when resolving cases. Written documents, though less common than in Roman times, remained important for recording land grants and legal decisions.

Justice and Trial Procedures
Trial by ordeal—such as carrying a hot iron or retrieving a stone from boiling water—became an accepted method to determine guilt or innocence. This practice was rooted in the belief that God would protect the innocent from harm. While these tests might seem brutal, they were part of the cultural fusion of Christian faith and Germanic custom in Merovingian courts.

---

6. Cultural Life and Daily Realities

Merovingian Gaul saw a mix of old Roman urban traditions, new Frankish influences, and Christian values. This era is sometimes called a "Dark Age," but it still had cultural vitality, especially within the church and monastic communities.

Urban versus Rural
Cities, once thriving under Rome, shrank in size. Many people moved to the countryside for safety or to work on large estates (villae). Still, cities like Paris, Reims, and Tours remained centers of religious and political activity, hosting cathedrals and royal courts. Rural areas were dominated by agriculture, with peasants (coloni, tenants, or free farmers) working the fields.

Art and Architecture
Merovingian art shows a strong Germanic influence in metalwork (jewelry, weapon decorations) and a continued Roman influence in stone sculpture and church design. Monasteries and churches sponsored illuminated manuscripts, though fewer survive compared to later medieval times. Wooden buildings, often with

thatched roofs, were the norm for most people. Stone construction was reserved for significant sites, like cathedrals or major royal residences.

Literacy and Learning
Literacy rates were low outside the clergy and upper nobility. However, some schools existed in cathedrals and monasteries, preserving Latin texts and teaching reading, writing, and basic religious knowledge. Bishops like Gregory of Tours (6th century) wrote historical works—most famously his *History of the Franks*—which provides vital insight into Merovingian society.

Trade and Economy
Long-distance trade declined from the heights of the Roman period but never disappeared. Some routes connecting the Mediterranean to northern Gaul remained active, bringing goods like wine and olive oil. Coastal and river trade also continued. Local markets were key for everyday goods. Barter was common, but coins—especially gold coins minted in royal mints—circulated among the wealthier classes.

---

7. The Mayors of the Palace and the Decline of Merovingian Power

As the 7th century progressed, real authority in the Frankish kingdoms shifted from the Merovingian kings to the mayors of the palace (*maiores palatii*). These officials originally managed the royal household, but over time, they assumed broader administrative and military powers.

Origins of the Mayor of the Palace
Each Merovingian sub-kingdom had its own mayor of the palace, responsible for overseeing court personnel, managing royal estates, and sometimes directing the army. When kings were minors or weak, the mayor acted as a regent. Powerful mayors used this position to control access to the king and distribute patronage to allies.

Rise of the Arnulfing-Pippinid Family
One family in Austrasia, known as the Arnulfings (after Bishop Arnulf of Metz) and the Pippinids (after Pepin of Landen), rose to dominate the mayoral office. By forging alliances with other noble families and the church, they gained vast

landholdings and military support. Eventually, leaders like Pepin of Herstal (sometimes called Pepin II) united Austrasia, Neustria, and Burgundy under their control, even though a Merovingian king still nominally ruled.

"Do-Nothing Kings"

As the mayors consolidated power, the later Merovingian kings, often referred to by historians as the "rois fainéants" or "do-nothing kings," became figureheads. They still held the title of rex (king), but the real political and military decisions were made by the mayor. This shift marked the final phase of Merovingian decline.

---

8. Pepin of Herstal, Charles Martel, and the Path to Carolingian Rule

Pepin of Herstal (Pepin II) was mayor of the palace in Austrasia from 687 CE and effectively ruled much of the Frankish realm until his death in 714. He passed on his power to his descendants, including Charles Martel, who would further strengthen the family's grip.

Pepin of Herstal's Achievements

- He united Austrasia and Neustria under his authority after defeating Neustrian rivals.
- He reduced the Merovingian king to a mere puppet.
- He maintained strong alliances with the church, granting lands to monasteries and bishoprics.

Charles Martel ("The Hammer")

Charles Martel, an illegitimate son of Pepin, seized control after a brief power struggle following his father's death. He became the de facto ruler from 718 CE onward. Charles is famously known for his victory at the Battle of Tours (or Poitiers) in 732, where he halted a raiding force of Muslim armies from Iberia. While the scale of that battle is debated by modern historians, it still solidified Charles Martel's reputation as a champion of Christendom.

Charles restructured the Frankish military by granting land (benefices) to warriors in return for service. This helped create a more stable cavalry force, laying early foundations for a feudal-like system. By the time of his death in 741, Charles Martel had firmly established the rule of his family line.

Transition to a New Dynasty
Charles's sons, Carloman and Pepin the Short, succeeded him as mayors of the palace. They continued to keep a Merovingian king on the throne for a while, but the facade wore thin. Pepin the Short eventually took a bold step that would end Merovingian rule and inaugurate the Carolingian dynasty.

---

9. End of the Merovingian Line

The last Merovingian king, Childeric III, had no real authority. Pepin the Short, seeking a legitimate way to claim the royal title, turned to the Pope. In 751, Pope Zachary agreed that whoever held real power should be king. This decision effectively sanctioned the deposition of Childeric III. Pepin was then anointed and crowned, marking the official transition to the Carolingian dynasty.

Why the Pope Supported Pepin
The papacy needed protection against the Lombards in Italy, and Pepin was a strong military leader. By supporting Pepin's claim, the Pope secured an alliance that would later prove critical for defending Rome. This cooperation between the Frankish ruler and the Pope would grow even stronger under Pepin's son, Charlemagne, setting a precedent for medieval kingship that linked earthly and spiritual power.

Legacy of the Merovingians
Though deposed, the Merovingians left a lasting imprint on the region. They bridged the gap between late Roman Gaul and the medieval world. They introduced or preserved legal traditions, supported the Christianization of the population, and laid the groundwork for the feudal structures that would characterize Europe for centuries. Their rule was marked by conflict and fragmentation, but also by cultural adaptation and resilience.

10. Merovingian Contributions to the Shaping of Early Medieval France

Despite their often-chaotic reign, the Merovingians oversaw several key developments:

1. **Christian Identity**: Clovis's conversion and subsequent royal patronage ensured the church's central role. This helped unify the population under a shared faith and a growing ecclesiastical network.
2. **Legal Fusion**: The coexistence of Salic Law with Roman legal traditions helped shape early medieval law codes, providing a basis for justice systems that blended Germanic custom with Roman heritage.
3. **Urban and Rural Life**: Though many Roman cities declined, they remained important centers for bishops and local governance. Meanwhile, the countryside witnessed the evolution of large estates.
4. **Noble Power**: Merovingian fragmentation allowed aristocratic families and mayors of the palace to gain influence. Over time, these figures would become the backbone of feudalism.
5. **Cultural Mix**: Gallo-Roman, Frankish, and Christian elements merged into a new social and cultural identity. The seeds of the French language (from evolving Latin dialects) and the future shape of French society can be traced to this era.

By the middle of the 8th century, the Merovingians had run out of momentum. Their decline opened the door for the Carolingians—descendants of Charles Martel—to bring new energy and consolidation. Yet, the Merovingian foundation was critical. Without it, the Carolingians might not have found such strong support or a unified territorial base to build upon.

CHAPTER 6: THE CAROLINGIAN DYNASTY AND THE REIGN OF CHARLEMAGNE

Introduction

The transition from Merovingian to Carolingian rule marked a turning point in the history of Gaul (now evolving into a distinct entity we can call France, though that exact term was not yet in use). Pepin the Short's coronation in 751 CE inaugurated a dynasty that would reach its zenith under his son, Charlemagne (Charles the Great). During Charlemagne's reign, the Carolingian Empire encompassed much of Western and Central Europe, uniting diverse peoples under one crown and a revived sense of imperial destiny.

In this chapter, we will explore how the Carolingians rose to power, focusing on Pepin the Short's reforms and conquests, then delve into Charlemagne's expansive campaigns, administrative structures, relationship with the papacy, and cultural achievements. We will see how the so-called "Carolingian Renaissance" had a long-lasting impact on education, art, and church organization. By the time Charlemagne died in 814 CE, he had redrawn the political map of Europe and laid down roots that would shape medieval kingdoms for centuries.

1. Pepin the Short

Pepin the Short (reigned 751–768) was the first Carolingian king, but he came to power after a careful negotiation with the papacy. This moment was not just a local shift; it signaled a new concept of kingship linked closely with the Church of Rome.

Deposition of the Last Merovingian
After securing papal backing, Pepin deposed Childeric III and took the throne. In 754, Pope Stephen II traveled to the Frankish kingdom and anointed Pepin in a ceremony that emphasized his sacred right to rule. This act laid the groundwork

for the idea that kings were chosen by God, using anointing with holy oil as a symbol of divine sanction.

Military Campaigns and the Donation of Pepin
Pepin proved himself a capable military leader, especially in Italy. At the pope's request, he defeated the Lombards threatening Rome. In a famous act known as the "Donation of Pepin," he granted certain lands in central Italy to the papacy, effectively creating the Papal States. This solidified the Frankish alliance with the pope, setting a precedent of cooperation between the Carolingians and the Church that would only grow under Charlemagne.

Internal Reforms
Pepin also worked to strengthen royal authority within the Frankish realm. He reformed the coinage system, standardizing weights and measures to facilitate trade. He used assemblies (placita) of local nobles and bishops to pass laws and ensure loyalty. Royal agents (missi dominici) began to appear as inspectors or envoys, traveling the kingdom to enforce the king's decrees—an idea Charlemagne would expand.

Family and Succession
Pepin married Bertrada of Laon, and they had sons, including Charles (later Charlemagne) and Carloman. Upon Pepin's death in 768, he divided the kingdom between them, following Frankish custom. Carloman died in 771, leaving Charlemagne as the sole ruler, thus preventing another round of partition that might have weakened the kingdom.

---

2. Charlemagne's Accession and Early Campaigns

When Charlemagne inherited his father's throne, he was around 24 years old. From the start, he showed ambitions for expansion and consolidation, viewing himself not just as a king but as a protector of Christianity.

Reunification of the Frankish Kingdom
The unexpected death of Carloman in 771 removed the immediate threat of a divided kingdom. Charlemagne quickly took control of Carloman's territory, sidelining Carloman's heirs with little opposition from the nobility. This gave Charlemagne a strong, unified base of power in Gaul and beyond.

War Against the Lombards

Like his father, Charlemagne soon found himself drawn to Italy. In 773–774, responding to calls for help from Pope Adrian I, he marched against the Lombards, whose king, Desiderius, threatened papal interests. Charlemagne's forces won decisively, and he took the title "King of the Lombards." This direct kingship over another people was unusual for a Frankish ruler and signaled Charlemagne's growing sense of imperial mission.

Campaigns in Saxony

One of Charlemagne's longest and most brutal wars was the conflict with the Saxons, a pagan Germanic people northeast of Frankish lands. From 772 to roughly 804, Charlemagne conducted multiple campaigns, aiming not only to subdue the Saxons but also to convert them to Christianity. He set up missionary bishoprics, destroyed pagan sanctuaries, and imposed harsh measures (such as the Capitulatio de partibus Saxoniae) that penalized pagan practices with death. The Saxon wars were costly and protracted, but they extended Frankish control deep into Germanic territory.

---

3. The Expansion of the Carolingian Realm

Under Charlemagne, the Frankish kingdom evolved into an empire stretching across large parts of Western and Central Europe. His military ventures were not always driven by pure conquest; many had a religious motive or were cast as defensive actions, though expansion certainly benefited Frankish nobility and the church with new lands and resources.

Bavaria and the Avars

In the late 8th century, Charlemagne turned his attention to Bavaria, whose duke, Tassilo III, had grown increasingly independent. Charlemagne deposed Tassilo in 788, incorporating Bavaria fully into the realm. This gave the Franks a strategic launching point to attack the Avars, a steppe people who had formed a powerful confederation along the Danube.

Between 791 and the early 800s, Carolingian armies campaigned against the Avars. The Franks ultimately dismantled the Avar Ring, a fortified encampment holding vast treasures. The Avars never recovered their former power, and Charlemagne's influence reached the edges of the Hungarian plains.

Spanish March

To the southwest, Charlemagne attempted to push Muslim forces back across the Pyrenees. In 778, he led an expedition into the Iberian Peninsula, an effort that included the famous Battle of Roncevaux Pass (778), where Basque fighters ambushed his rearguard, killing several notable Frankish nobles including Roland. Though the campaign was not entirely successful, Charlemagne established a buffer zone in what is now Catalonia, known as the Spanish March, securing the southern boundary of his empire.

Overall Impact

By around 800 CE, Charlemagne's empire encompassed present-day France, Belgium, the Netherlands, Switzerland, large parts of Germany and Austria, northern and central Italy, and small sections of Spain. This was the largest European political unit since the fall of the Western Roman Empire. It provided a measure of stability and revived the idea that a single Christian ruler could govern a vast territory under divine sanction.

---

4. Administration and the Missi Dominici

Ruling such an expansive realm required effective administration. Charlemagne built on Pepin's reforms, expanding the role of the *missi dominici* ("the lord's envoys"). These pairs of officials—usually a bishop and a lay noble—traveled through designated regions to oversee local counts, ensure justice, and collect royal revenues.

Counts and Dukes

Local governance was entrusted to counts (comites) and, in some frontier regions, dukes. They held judicial, military, and administrative powers. However, Charlemagne sought to keep them in check by:

- **Requiring oaths of loyalty**: All local officials had to swear fealty.
- **Rotating or removing counts**: He sometimes transferred them to different regions to prevent entrenched local dynasties.
- **Using royal agents (missi dominici)**: These traveling inspectors reported back to the king any abuse of power.

Capitularies and Royal Decrees

Charlemagne issued *capitularies*, written decrees covering diverse matters such as church reform, judicial procedures, coinage standards, and moral conduct. They were read aloud in assemblies so that local lords and clergy understood the king's directives. Even if literacy was limited among the general populace, the public reading of these laws helped ensure some level of compliance.

Royal Assemblies

Like previous Frankish kings, Charlemagne held general assemblies in the spring or summer, where nobles, bishops, and abbots gathered. These meetings discussed wars, reforms, and legislation. By engaging major stakeholders, Charlemagne managed to secure cooperation for his far-reaching policies.

---

5. The Relationship with the Papacy and the Imperial Coronation

A pivotal moment in Charlemagne's reign was his coronation as "Emperor of the Romans" by Pope Leo III on Christmas Day, 800 CE, in St. Peter's Basilica, Rome. This event reintroduced a Western Roman Empire in the eyes of many contemporaries, even though the Eastern Roman Empire (Byzantium) in Constantinople still existed.

Alliance with Pope Leo III

Pope Leo III faced internal opposition in Rome. Accused of various crimes by Roman nobility, he sought Charlemagne's protection. After the Frankish king intervened, Leo III was restored to power. To show gratitude—and perhaps to establish a new political order—he crowned Charlemagne emperor.

Significance of the Coronation

1. **Revival of the Imperial Title**: Since the deposition of the last Western Emperor in 476, the imperial title in the West had been vacant. Charlemagne's coronation symbolized a Christian renewal of the Roman Empire in Western Europe.
2. **Papal Authority**: By crowning Charlemagne, the pope underscored his own power to grant (or at least proclaim) the imperial title. This act laid groundwork for future debates over whether the emperor was supreme over the pope or vice versa.

3. **Legitimacy and Prestige**: The imperial crown gave Charlemagne increased prestige among European elites. It helped him negotiate with the Byzantine Empire, which only gradually recognized his new title.

Charlemagne may not have fully welcomed the idea that his authority derived from a papal ceremony—there are indications he felt somewhat surprised or ambivalent at the event—but it undoubtedly strengthened the symbolic bond between the Carolingian monarchy and the Church.

---

6. The Carolingian Renaissance

One of the most enduring legacies of Charlemagne's reign was the cultural revival commonly called the Carolingian Renaissance. It was not a full "rebirth" in the sense of later Renaissance periods, but rather a focused effort to promote learning, reform religious practices, and standardize writing.

Educational Reforms
Charlemagne recognized that the clergy often lacked basic literacy, which he saw as a threat to correct Christian teaching. He invited scholars from across Europe, such as Alcuin of York and Paul the Deacon, to his court at Aachen (Aix-la-Chapelle). They established schools in monasteries and cathedrals, teaching the liberal arts (grammar, rhetoric, logic, arithmetic, geometry, music, and astronomy) and encouraging scriptural study.

Script and Manuscript Production
A major innovation was the development of the Carolingian minuscule script, a clear and uniform style of handwriting. This script made reading and copying texts easier, helping preserve many classical Latin works. Scribes in monasteries produced illuminated manuscripts, often with decorative initials and simple but elegant designs. The improved legibility of Carolingian minuscule had a long-lasting impact; much of our current Latin alphabet style traces back to it.

Liturgical and Theological Standardization
To unify worship across his empire, Charlemagne promoted the Roman liturgy over local Gallican rites. He also supported the collection and study of canon law. Scholars at his court debated theological issues, aiming to clarify doctrines and eliminate what the king and his advisors deemed heretical or erroneous.

Architecture and Art
Charlemagne's palace chapel at Aachen is the most famous architectural legacy. Inspired by Byzantine and classical models, it combined a central octagonal plan with rich mosaics. Art from this period featured Christian themes, reflecting Charlemagne's vision of a unified Christian empire. The imperial court sponsored metalwork, sculpture, and ivory carvings, though fewer examples survive compared to manuscripts.

---

7. Social and Economic Structures under Charlemagne

Charlemagne's empire still resembled a patchwork of local economies and traditions, but the king tried to set overarching standards.

Land and Lordship
As in Merovingian times, land was key to power. Charlemagne rewarded loyal nobles with estates or allowed them to keep their ancestral holdings, in return for providing soldiers and managing local governance. The concept of vassalage strengthened: nobles swore fealty to the king in exchange for protection and resources.

Agriculture and Trade
Most people lived on rural estates, producing grains, livestock, and limited surpluses. Market towns existed, but large-scale trade was more limited than in Roman times. Still, Charlemagne's coinage reform helped stabilize currency, and certain trade routes—especially for luxury goods like textiles, metals, and spices—remained active. Coastal and river networks also facilitated movement of goods.

Urban Centers
Cities such as Paris, Lyon, and Bordeaux were far smaller than they had been under Rome, but they served as regional hubs. Aachen itself grew as the imperial capital, hosting the royal court, palace complex, and chapel. Charlemagne spent much of his reign traveling (the "itinerant court"), ensuring personal oversight of the empire's diverse regions.

Serfdom and Peasantry

While outright slavery had diminished, serfdom bound peasants to the land. Serfs were not free; they owed labor and dues to their lords, though they did retain some legal rights. Free peasants existed as well, often working smaller plots. The distinction between serf and free peasant could be fluid, influenced by local customs, debts, and the need for protection.

---

8. The Later Years of Charlemagne's Reign

As Charlemagne aged, he dealt with ongoing conflicts and the complexity of governing a massive empire. He fought additional campaigns in Saxony, the eastern frontiers, and in northern Spain, though by this time the empire's boundaries were largely set.

Succession Planning

Charlemagne's original plan involved dividing his empire among his sons. However, all but one of them predeceased him. Eventually, he crowned his surviving son, Louis (later known as Louis the Pious), as co-emperor in 813. This act aimed to ensure a smooth transition, unlike the partitions that often tore Merovingian realms apart.

Imperial Administration

Even in his later years, Charlemagne continued to issue capitularies, refine coinage, and send out missi dominici. He was keenly aware that the empire's stability depended on strong leadership and cooperation with the nobility and church. He also encouraged the conversion and pacification of frontier regions, though these efforts met with mixed success.

Diplomacy with Byzantium and the Caliphate

Charlemagne maintained diplomatic contacts beyond his immediate borders. He sent emissaries to the Byzantine court, negotiating recognition of his imperial title, and exchanged gifts with the Abbasid Caliph Harun al-Rashid. These diplomatic relationships brought exotic goods to the Carolingian court and reinforced Charlemagne's image as a major ruler on the European stage.

9. Death of Charlemagne and the Aftermath

Charlemagne died in 814, in Aachen, at around age 71. He left behind an empire that was large, diverse, and held together by a combination of personal authority, military force, and a shared Christian identity.

Succession by Louis the Pious
Louis the Pious inherited the imperial crown. Though he was a devout Christian, his reign faced internal rebellions, noble revolts, and power struggles among his sons. Over time, these conflicts weakened the cohesion of the empire. Eventually, the Treaty of Verdun in 843 split the realm among Louis's surviving sons, forming precursor territories that would evolve into France, Germany, and northern Italy.

Charlemagne's Legacy
Charlemagne's reign is often viewed as a formative period for Western Europe. Key aspects of his legacy include:

1. **Strengthened Ties to the Papacy**: His coronation and subsequent relationship with the pope became a model for future medieval kings.
2. **Cultural Revival**: The Carolingian Renaissance preserved ancient texts and improved education for the clergy and nobility.
3. **Administrative Framework**: The system of counts, dukes, and missi dominici offered a template for later medieval governance.
4. **Christian Empire**: His campaigns helped spread Christianity in Europe, though often by force.
5. **Dynastic Model**: The idea of an emperor overseeing multiple kingdoms under a single faith influenced later concepts of a Holy Roman Empire.

---

10. The Formation of a Medieval Identity

Under Charlemagne and the Carolingians, the territories once known as Gaul took on a clearer shape in the context of Europe. Latin culture, now heavily Christianized, merged with Germanic traditions. The seeds of the French language grew in the northern part of the empire as Latin evolved in local dialects. Noble families solidified their positions, and monastic centers blossomed as guardians of literacy and learning.

Transition Toward Feudal Structures

Though a fully defined feudal system would emerge more clearly in the 9th and 10th centuries, its roots were visible under Charlemagne. The bond between a lord and vassal, cemented by land grants, became the norm for raising military forces. Royal authority was strong during Charlemagne's reign but depended heavily on personal leadership and success in battle. When that strong hand was gone, power diffused among magnates.

Influence on Future French Kingship

Later French monarchs would claim spiritual and cultural descent from Charlemagne. Even as the empire fractured, the western portion—eventually called West Francia—would evolve into the Kingdom of France. The Carolingian memory provided legitimacy to rulers seeking to connect their authority to Charlemagne's empire-building achievements.

Cultural Continuity

From coinage reforms to the standardization of Christian rites, Charlemagne's policies lingered. Libraries in monastic houses kept copies of classical and Christian texts. Artistic styles influenced later medieval manuscript illumination and church architecture. Although the empire divided, many Carolingian innovations shaped local governance and cultural life for centuries.

CHAPTER 7: THE FRAGMENTATION OF POWER AND THE FEUDAL SYSTEM

Introduction

After Charlemagne's death in 814, his son Louis the Pious inherited a vast empire that stretched across much of Western and Central Europe. However, internal divisions and external pressures soon weakened this grand realm. By the mid-9th century, the Carolingian Empire was fracturing into distinct political units. At the same time, a new way of structuring society, which we call "feudalism," was taking shape. This system rested on bonds of loyalty between lords and vassals, tied together by grants of land called fiefs.

In this chapter, we will examine how Charlemagne's empire fell apart under his successors, leading to civil wars and territorial splits. We will also explore the Viking raids, which devastated large parts of northern Gaul (France) and further eroded central authority. As the Carolingians lost their grip, local nobles gained more power, forging the regional principalities that set the stage for medieval France. Finally, we will discuss how these changes gave rise to feudal relationships and shaped daily life for nobles, knights, and peasants alike.

1. Louis the Pious and the Early Breakup of the Empire

Louis the Pious and His Challenges

Charlemagne crowned his only surviving son, Louis the Pious, as co-emperor in 813 to ensure a smooth succession. When Charlemagne died the following year, Louis inherited the entire Carolingian realm. Louis was a devout Christian who sought to uphold the empire's unity and religious standards. But he faced several obstacles:

1. **Family Rivalries**: Louis tried to arrange a fair division of the empire among his sons. However, shifting plans and the birth of a fourth son from a second marriage led to conflict among the royal heirs.
2. **Noble Power**: High-ranking nobles expected rewards—land, titles, influence—for supporting one or another prince. Their shifting allegiances fueled political instability.
3. **Rebellions**: Louis's sons rebelled more than once, hoping to secure larger shares of the empire or greater independence. The divisions weakened the central authority Louis had inherited.

Ordinatio Imperii (817)

Early in his reign, Louis issued an imperial decree called the *Ordinatio Imperii*. It was an attempt to preserve the empire's integrity by designating his eldest son, Lothair, as co-emperor and primary heir. His other sons, Pepin and Louis the German, would be subordinate kings in specific regions. But later changes—especially the birth of Charles the Bald (a son by Louis's second wife)—disrupted this plan. Louis tried to find new arrangements to include Charles, sparking fresh disputes among all four sons.

Civil War and Weakening of Authority

Between 829 and 833, Louis faced multiple uprisings from his sons. At one point, he was even deposed and forced to do public penance. Though he returned to power, the repeated rebellions created lingering distrust. Nobles and bishops took sides, leading to ongoing turmoil. By the time of Louis the Pious's death in 840, the empire had been thoroughly shaken by internal strife. The unity Charlemagne had worked so hard to build was unraveling.

---

2. The Treaty of Verdun (843) and Its Impact

Struggle Among Louis's Sons

After Louis the Pious died, his surviving sons—Lothair, Louis the German, and Charles the Bald—immediately fell into open warfare over the empire. The decisive conflict was the Battle of Fontenoy in 841, where Charles and Louis the German joined forces to defeat Lothair. However, continued fighting drove the brothers to seek a compromise.

The Treaty of Verdun (843)

In 843, the three brothers negotiated the Treaty of Verdun, effectively partitioning the Carolingian Empire into three main realms:

1. **Lothair I**: Retained the imperial title and the middle kingdom, stretching from the North Sea down through the Rhine Valley into Italy (sometimes called Lotharingia).
2. **Louis the German**: Took control of East Francia, which would evolve into parts of modern Germany.
3. **Charles the Bald**: Ruled West Francia, roughly corresponding to much of modern France, extending from the Atlantic coast eastward to a fluid boundary with Lothair's territory.

This division is often seen as a key moment in the creation of separate cultural-linguistic zones that foreshadowed the future nations of France and Germany. For our narrative, the western kingdom under Charles the Bald is the direct predecessor of medieval France.

Continued Fragmentation

The Treaty of Verdun did not bring lasting peace. Lothair's middle kingdom was awkwardly shaped and vulnerable to further splits. Successive treaties, such as the Treaty of Prüm (855) and the Treaty of Mersen (870), subdivided territories further upon each ruler's death. As royal domains shrank and changed hands, local counts and dukes exploited the chaos to expand their power. West Francia (the western realm) likewise went through multiple partitions and contested successions, contributing to the gradual erosion of effective royal authority.

---

3. Viking Raids and the Erosion of Central Power

Origins of the Viking Threat

Starting in the late 8th century, Scandinavians—often called Vikings or Northmen—raided the coasts of England, Ireland, and the Carolingian Empire. By the mid-9th century, these raids were frequent in West Francia. Vikings navigated up the Seine, the Loire, and other rivers, attacking monasteries and cities for loot. They capitalized on the region's political instability, knowing that local forces were often too scattered to mount a strong defense.

Notable Viking Attacks

- In **845**, a Viking fleet led by the legendary warlord Ragnar Lothbrok (according to some sources) raided Paris. Charles the Bald paid a large ransom to make them leave, setting a precedent for future payments.
- Throughout the **850s** and **860s**, Vikings established winter camps along riverbanks. They used these bases to strike deeper into the countryside, forcing counts and bishops to buy peace through tribute or to hastily build fortifications.

Impact on the Realm
The Viking threat accelerated the decline in royal authority. Charles the Bald and later kings lacked sufficient standing armies to protect all regions, so they relied on local lords to organize defense. Over time, these lords fortified their strongholds, trained their own knights, and negotiated independently with raiders. As a result, power shifted away from the king to regional magnates who could offer protection.

Birth of Normandy
One significant outcome of the Viking presence was the creation of the Duchy of Normandy. In **911**, Charles the Simple granted lands around the lower Seine to a Viking leader, Rollo, in exchange for protection against other raiders. This arrangement—recorded in the Treaty of Saint-Clair-sur-Epte—illustrates how royal authority negotiated with invaders and transformed them into vassals. Normandy thus became a powerful principality, governed by Norse rulers who adopted Christianity and the local language over generations.

---

4. The Rise of Local Lords and the Decline of Carolingian Kings

Weak Successors and Regional Independence
Following Charles the Bald's death (877), West Francia saw a rapid succession of kings, many of whom were weak or preoccupied with internal conflicts. Some Carolingian rulers faced deposition by noble factions. Counts, dukes, and viscounts—once mere royal appointees—started acting like independent princes, passing their titles to heirs and building alliances through marriage.

Count Odo and the Siege of Paris (885–886)
The Siege of Paris by Vikings in 885–886 was a turning point. Count Odo (or Eudes),

a member of the Robertian family, took charge of the city's defense. His leadership won him widespread fame. When the reigning king, Charles the Fat, failed to provide decisive relief, nobles in West Francia lost confidence in the Carolingian line. After Charles the Fat's deposition, they elected Odo as king in 888. Although a Carolingian (Charles the Simple) eventually returned to power, Odo's reign showed that influential lords could seize the crown independently.

Robertians and Other Powerful Families

The Robertian family, which included Odo and his brother Robert I, gained major influence. They controlled large swaths of territory in northern France. Similar families in other regions—like the Counts of Flanders, the Dukes of Aquitaine, and the Counts of Toulouse—solidified their hold over local lands. This network of semi-independent principalities shaped the political map of West Francia in the 9th and 10th centuries.

Struggles Over the Throne

Between 888 and 987, the West Frankish throne changed hands multiple times between Carolingians and non-Carolingians (like the Robertians). The real power often lay in the baronial and ducal courts, where lords commanded knights and managed local economies. By the 10th century, the once-mighty Carolingian dynasty was a shadow of its former self, heavily reliant on the support of regional magnates to maintain even a semblance of royal authority.

---

5. Defining Feudalism

Origins of Feudal Structures

The term "feudalism" is modern, but it describes a set of practices that evolved in this period. As royal power declined, local defense and governance became the responsibility of land-owning nobles. To maintain armies, these nobles granted land (fiefs) to warriors (vassals) in exchange for military service and loyalty. The arrangement provided protection and structure in a time of uncertainty.

Vassalage

At the heart of feudalism lay the personal bond called "vassalage." A man became a vassal by kneeling before a lord, placing his hands within the lord's hands, and swearing an oath of fealty. In return, the lord promised to protect the vassal and grant him a piece of land or income. This ceremony was both legal and symbolic, establishing mutual obligations.

Fiefs (Benefices)

A fief was usually a piece of land, though it could also involve rights to collect taxes or tolls. The vassal managed the fief, collected its revenues, and used a portion to equip himself as a knight (a mounted warrior). He also provided troops (often a small retinue of armed men) for the lord's military campaigns. If a vassal died, his heir typically had to renew the oath and might pay a fee (relief) to inherit the fief.

Feudal Hierarchies

Feudal relationships created a hierarchy, with the king notionally at the top. Below him sat the great dukes and counts, who were themselves lords to lesser nobles. Those lesser nobles could, in turn, have vassals of their own. This chain of lord-vassal ties formed a patchwork of overlapping loyalties rather than a clear, centralized government. A count could be a vassal to the king, but also a lord to many knights.

Homage and the Complexity of Feudal Ties

Because multiple lords existed, a vassal might hold fiefs from different superiors, creating conflicting loyalties. This complexity often led to feudal warfare, as nobles balanced or betrayed allegiances to gain advantage. The king, lacking a large standing army, had to negotiate with his powerful vassals continually.

---

6. Castles and the Militarization of the Countryside

Fortifications as Power Centers

The insecurity of the 9th and 10th centuries gave rise to a proliferation of castles. Initially, building a castle was a royal privilege, but many nobles constructed fortifications without royal approval. A castle served as both a residence and a defensive stronghold, typically surrounded by walls, a moat, or other obstacles. From these strongholds, local lords controlled surrounding lands, collected taxes, and enforced laws.

Stone Keeps and Motte-and-Bailey Castles

Early castles often started as wooden fortifications called *motte-and-bailey*:

1. **Motte**: A raised earth mound with a wooden tower on top.
2. **Bailey**: An enclosed courtyard at the base of the motte, protected by a wooden fence or palisade.
   Over time, wealthier lords replaced these wooden structures with stone

keeps and more elaborate walls. The shift to stone significantly increased defensive strength, making castles formidable centers of power.

Castle Lords and Their Retinues
Each castle was home to the lord, his family, and a retinue of knights or armed retainers. In exchange for land or pay, these knights provided the lord with military service. They often trained locally, practicing mounted combat and participating in small-scale conflicts. Over generations, a knightly class emerged, defined by codes of loyalty and martial skill.

Impact on Peasants
For peasants living near a castle, the local lord provided some measure of protection against raiders or rival lords—though at a price. Peasants owed labor, taxes (in produce or coin), and fees for using the lord's mill or oven. They also faced the risk of being caught up in feudal warfare if their lord clashed with a neighboring baron. Castles solidified the nobles' grip on rural communities, often isolating peasants from any direct royal administration.

---

7. The Church in a Fragmented World

Church as a Landowner
Alongside secular lords, the church was a major landholder. Monasteries and bishoprics received grants of land from kings and nobles, turning abbots and bishops into significant feudal lords themselves. They employed knights to defend ecclesiastical property. Some bishops oversaw large territories, competing with secular counts for dominance in local affairs.

Reform Movements
By the 10th century, parts of the church sought to free clerical institutions from the entanglements of feudal lordship. Noble families often dominated bishoprics or monasteries, appointing relatives to church offices. The **Cluniac Reform**, originating at the Abbey of Cluny (founded in 910), aimed to end such secular interference, emphasizing stricter religious discipline and papal authority. Over time, these reforms contributed to a reevaluation of the church's role in feudal society.

Peacemaking Efforts: Truce of God and Peace of God
In regions wracked by feudal warfare, church leaders initiated movements like the

Peace of God (Pax Dei) and **Truce of God** (Treuga Dei). These proclaimed that certain times (holy days, Sundays) and places (churches, monasteries) were off-limits for violence. They also tried to protect non-combatants, such as peasants and clergy. While not always successful, these initiatives reflected the church's attempt to limit perpetual conflict and encourage stability.

Pilgrimages and Relic Cults

Even amid fragmentation, religious devotion flourished. Pilgrimages to holy sites—like Rome, Santiago de Compostela, or local shrines—helped connect distant regions. The veneration of saints' relics grew, with abbeys and cathedrals competing to attract pilgrims. These shrines became spiritual and economic hubs, sometimes fostering the growth of nearby towns.

---

8. Everyday Life Under Feudalism

Peasants and Serfs

Most of the population were peasants. Some were free, able to move and own land, but many were serfs bound to the lord's manor. Serfs needed the lord's permission to marry or leave the estate. In return, they received small plots to farm for their families, plus protection in times of war. Life was hard, with long labor on fields, limited diets, and vulnerabilities to famine, disease, and warfare.

Manorial Organization

Manorialism was closely tied to feudalism. A manor typically consisted of the lord's demesne (land farmed for the lord's benefit) plus peasant holdings. Peasants owed labor services—like plowing the lord's fields a certain number of days each week—or paid rent in produce. The manor had a mill, bakery, and other facilities that peasants were required to use for a fee. This system ensured local self-sufficiency, though it could be oppressive for the lower classes.

Knights and Warfare

Knights were the military elite. Training in mounted combat, they used lances, swords, and shields. Over time, chainmail armor (and later plate armor) enhanced their protection. While knights were a step above peasants in status, many lived modestly, reliant on their fief's income. Major lords might field hundreds of knights for a campaign, but day-to-day violence was localized—raids, small-scale sieges, and feuds.

Women in Feudal Society

Women in noble families could inherit land if there was no direct male heir, making them valuable in marriage alliances. Some noblewomen managed estates, especially while husbands or fathers went to war. However, they generally had fewer legal rights and remained under the guardianship of male relatives. In monasteries, nuns sometimes held authority—an abbess could wield significant power over an abbey's lands.

---

9. Transition to the Capetian Era

Decline of the Last Carolingians

By the late 10th century, the Carolingian line in West Francia was nearly extinct. Kings like Louis V, known as "Louis the Lazy," held little sway outside their immediate domains. The Robertian dukes and other powerful nobles essentially controlled the kingdom. When Louis V died childless in 987, a council of Frankish magnates convened to choose his successor.

Election of Hugh Capet (987)

That council selected Hugh Capet, a Robertian duke and grandson of King Robert I, as king. The choice was largely symbolic—Hugh was already a leading noble in the region around Paris and Orléans. His coronation marked the end of Carolingian rule in West Francia and the start of the Capetian Dynasty. At the time, few predicted how enduring the Capetian line would be.

Challenges Facing Hugh Capet

Hugh's royal domain was small, mostly limited to the lands around Paris (the Île-de-France). Many great lords—like the dukes of Normandy, Brittany, Aquitaine, and Burgundy—were practically independent. Hugh's initial reign was more about survival and establishing legitimacy than asserting strong central authority. Nonetheless, his crowning signified a shift toward a new royal house that would gradually reshape the realm.

Feudal Monarchy Emerges

Although the feudal order was well established, the monarchy did not disappear. Instead, it adapted. The early Capetians functioned as feudal lords in their own right, using feudal bonds to build alliances and occasionally asserting overlordship over weaker nobles. Over centuries, the Capetian kings would claw back power through strategic marriages, wars, and diplomacy. The seeds of a more centralized French kingdom were being planted.

---

10. Significance of the Feudal Age in Shaping Medieval France

A Stable Network Amid Chaos
Feudalism brought a degree of stability after the fragmentation of Carolingian authority. Local lords managed defense, justice, and economic life. Castles offered fortification, knights offered protection, and manors sustained the agricultural base. While violence was common, feudal structures provided a framework for organizing society in a world where central power was weak.

The Roots of French Identity
During this era, the cultural and linguistic differences between West Francia and other former Carolingian realms (like East Francia) deepened. Local dialects of Latin, later evolving into Old French, became more prominent in royal charters and everyday speech. Over time, these dialects would solidify into a distinct French language.

Long-Term Consequences
The fragmentation of power gave rise to principalities—Normandy, Anjou, Flanders, Burgundy, and Aquitaine, among others—that would play vital roles in later French history. The new Capetian kings, starting in 987, faced the daunting task of uniting these territories under a single crown. The church's continued presence as a landowner and moral authority also influenced how politics and society evolved, seeding future church-state tensions.

Looking Ahead
By 1000 CE, France was not yet the strong, centralized kingdom it would become. Instead, it was a mosaic of feudal lordships. The king had a royal title but controlled limited territory directly. Yet, the shift to Hugh Capet and the Capetian line would eventually transform the monarchy's power. As we move into the next chapter, we will see how the early Capetians expanded their influence step by step, forging the first real foundations of what we now call the Kingdom of France.

CHAPTER 8: THE CAPETIAN DYNASTY AND THE GROWTH OF ROYAL AUTHORITY

Introduction

In 987, Hugh Capet's coronation signaled the start of the Capetian Dynasty, which would eventually rule France for centuries. At the time of his ascension, however, the new king commanded limited resources and territory. Many of the great lords—such as the Dukes of Normandy and Aquitaine—were nearly as powerful as the king himself. The political map of France was a patchwork of feudal principalities, each guarded by its own castle networks and knightly retinues.

Over the following two centuries, the Capetian kings would gradually strengthen their position. They adopted innovative strategies—such as hereditary succession, alliances with the church, and strategic marriages—to assert greater control. These steps laid the foundation for the future expansion of royal power under figures like Philip II Augustus, Saint Louis (Louis IX), and beyond.

In this chapter, we will examine the early generations of Capetian rulers, from Hugh Capet through Louis VI and Louis VII. We will see how they coped with powerful vassals, forged ties with the papacy, and laid the groundwork for a more centralized monarchy. The process was slow and often met resistance from feudal magnates. Nonetheless, the Capetians steadily built the structures that would shape medieval France.

1. Hugh Capet and His Immediate Challenges

Limited Royal Domain
When Hugh Capet took the crown, his principal holdings were in the region of Paris and Orléans (the Île-de-France). This domain was relatively small compared to the vast territories held by some of his vassals. For instance:

- The **Dukes of Normandy** controlled a rich territory and had gained considerable wealth, partly from Viking roots and partly from tight governance.
- The **Counts of Anjou** were expanding southward and contesting parts of Maine and Touraine.
- The **Dukes of Aquitaine** ruled the expansive southwest, with resources from trade and agriculture.

Hugh's direct authority extended only so far as his own lands, and he had to rely on feudal ties to influence the rest of the kingdom.

Coronation and Hereditary Strategy
To secure his family's future, Hugh Capet had his son Robert crowned as co-king (associate king) during his own reign. This practice was not entirely new but became a hallmark of the early Capetians. By crowning an heir while the father still lived, the dynasty reduced the risk of contested succession after the king's death. It was a clever way to preserve continuity, ensuring that the title would stay within the Capetian line.

Relations with the Church
Hugh maintained a close alliance with the church, which viewed him favorably compared to the weaker, often conflict-ridden Carolingian successors. He supported monastic reform efforts (like Cluny) and granted privileges to bishoprics, hoping to secure moral backing for his fragile rule. Bishops, in turn, promoted the king's authority in their dioceses, though local magnates sometimes overrode even ecclesiastical influence.

Struggles Against Rival Lords
Early in his reign, Hugh faced challenges from Carolingian loyalists who supported Charles of Lorraine, a surviving member of the Carolingian house. However, Hugh managed to neutralize this threat and hold onto the throne. Still, his real power outside the Île-de-France remained limited. Much of his kingship involved subtle negotiation rather than overt conquest.

---

2. Robert II "the Pious" and Royal Legitimacy

Religious Reputation
Robert II, Hugh's son, inherited the crown without serious dispute—proof that the

co-kingship strategy had worked. Known as "the Pious" due to his devout nature, Robert II frequently clashed with church authorities over marital issues (he married within prohibited degrees of kinship) and was temporarily excommunicated. Yet his piety was also evident in generous donations to monasteries, promotion of liturgical music, and encouragement of church reforms.

Territorial Goals
Robert sought to extend his influence in Burgundy, where his mother came from. He laid claim to the Duchy of Burgundy and fought intermittent wars to assert control. Although he eventually secured part of that region, many local lords retained substantial autonomy. This struggle illustrated the difficulty of direct royal expansion: each region had entrenched noble families defending their rights.

Conflict with Noble Families
Robert dealt with multiple revolts, including opposition from Count Odo II of Blois, who controlled Champagne and other strategically important lands. The Count of Blois's domains often encircled the royal domain, making him a constant threat. Negotiation, marriage alliances, and occasional military campaigns were Robert's main tools for containing such powerful vassals.

Cultural Initiatives
Despite the political challenges, Robert's court became known for fostering clerical scholarship and liturgical development. Writers praised him as a moral example, though these praises sometimes glossed over his military failures and the complexities of his private life. Nonetheless, the association with devout kingship enhanced the Capetians' reputation as defenders of the faith, an image that future monarchs would cultivate.

---

3. Henry I and the Ongoing Feudal Struggle

Family Disputes
Henry I inherited the throne after Robert II, but his accession was not peaceful. Robert had favored another son, and the dispute nearly broke into open war. Eventually, Henry secured recognition by giving his brother Robert a strong position in Burgundy. These family quarrels underscored how fragile the royal line remained if multiple heirs contested the crown.

Rebellious Vassals

Even as king, Henry often found himself outmatched by powerful lords like the Duke of Normandy. By the mid-11th century, Normandy was rising quickly, especially under Duke William (later known as William the Conqueror). Henry intervened in Norman affairs, sometimes supporting Norman rebels against Duke William, but with mixed results. In time, William emerged stronger, and Henry had to accept his growing power.

Marriage Alliances

Henry married Anne of Kiev, a princess from a distant Rus' realm. This move was somewhat unusual, reflecting the Capetians' search for alliances that might strengthen their position without entangling them too closely with neighboring powers. The marriage produced royal heirs, including Philip I, ensuring the dynasty's continuation. However, it offered little immediate strategic advantage against domestic threats.

Limited Royal Authority

Like his predecessors, Henry had to navigate a kingdom fragmented by feudal custom. Each region boasted strong lords who resisted royal interference. Tax collection beyond the Île-de-France was minimal, and the king's courts did not regularly function in areas dominated by local counts or dukes. Yet, Henry maintained the idea of monarchy: he was an anointed king, chosen by God. That symbolic power was crucial, even if his day-to-day control was weak.

---

4. The Rise of Normandy and the Changing Balance of Power

Duke William of Normandy

During Henry I's reign, Duke William consolidated Normandy by crushing internal revolts. He then turned his gaze across the English Channel. In 1066, William launched the Norman Conquest of England, defeating King Harold Godwinson at the Battle of Hastings. He became William I (the Conqueror) of England, transforming Normandy into a cross-Channel powerhouse.

Impact on France

William's conquest added complexity to France's political scene. The Duke of Normandy was now also the King of England, making him, in theory, a vassal of the

French king for Normandy but an independent king in his English realm. This dual status would have enormous repercussions in later centuries, laying the groundwork for Anglo-French conflicts (such as the Norman-Angevin rivalries and, eventually, the Hundred Years' War).

Shift in Feudal Dynamics
With Normandy's ascendance, the Capetians faced a vassal whose resources from England far surpassed those of the French royal domain. King Philip I (Henry I's son) would have to deal with a neighbor who was sometimes both a subject and a rival. This reality exposed the Capetian monarchy's vulnerability, further highlighting the need to expand and consolidate royal power.

---

5. Philip I and Strategies for Survival

Minority and Regency
Philip I became king in 1060 at a young age, so his mother, Anne of Kiev, and her advisers initially governed. As Philip came of age, he had to contend with the looming power of the Norman-English realm. He also faced challenges from the Counts of Flanders and Anjou. Each of these principalities could field armies nearly as large as the king's.

Political Maneuvers
Philip used marriage alliances, diplomacy, and occasional military interventions to keep the peace—or at least prevent a total collapse of royal authority. One notable issue was Philip's controversial marriage to Bertrade of Montfort, which led to excommunication by Pope Urban II. This scandal damaged Philip's moral authority but did not dethrone him.

Growth of Royal Resources
Despite many setbacks, Philip managed to increase the royal domain slightly by acquiring territories through inheritance or strategic marriages. He also promoted the economic development of towns within his domain, granting charters that encouraged commerce. Over time, these towns (like Paris) became small but valuable sources of revenue and support for the crown.

Relations with the Church and the First Crusade
During Philip's reign, Pope Urban II called the First Crusade (1095), attracting many French nobles. Philip did not personally join due to his excommunication, but many

of his vassals, including notable lords from Normandy and elsewhere, participated. The Crusade affected the balance of power back home, as some nobles left to fight in the Holy Land, creating openings that Philip could exploit.

---

6. Louis VI "the Fat": Consolidation of Royal Power

Physical Presence and Administration
Louis VI earned the nickname "the Fat," partly due to his robust build, but he was known more for his active rule. Unlike some earlier Capetians, he constantly traveled his domain, asserting royal justice and challenging rebellious vassals. His chief advisor, Abbot Suger of Saint-Denis, played a crucial role in organizing and justifying royal authority.

Battles Against Raubritter (Robber Barons)
Many petty lords acted as robber barons, extorting travelers and terrorizing peasants. Louis VI launched campaigns to dismantle their castles or force them into submission. By doing so, he extended direct royal control in parts of the Île-de-France, making travel and trade safer and winning support from local towns.

Conflict with Henry I of England (Duke of Normandy)
King Henry I of England (William the Conqueror's son) was also Duke of Normandy. Louis VI contested Henry's influence over French affairs. Although Louis lacked the resources to mount a large-scale invasion of Normandy, he supported Norman rebels and fought skirmishes to assert his feudal overlordship. These conflicts were a precursor to later, more extensive Anglo-French rivalries.

Support from the Towns
Louis VI recognized the growing importance of urban centers. He granted privileges or "communes" to certain towns, allowing them some self-governance in return for taxes and loyalty. These towns became allies in the king's efforts to contain powerful nobles. A city charter often included the right to hold markets, build walls, and form local militias, aiding both economic growth and regional security.

Royal Administration and Abbot Suger
Abbot Suger served as a key royal administrator, diplomat, and propagandist. He wrote favorably of Louis VI's deeds, shaping the king's reputation as a just ruler. Suger also supervised the rebuilding of the Abbey of Saint-Denis, pioneering the

early Gothic style in architecture. This close partnership between a king and a leading churchman foreshadowed later strategies of centralization, where the monarchy and the church worked in tandem—though often not without tension.

---

7. Louis VII: Marital Alliances and Early Conflicts

Marriage to Eleanor of Aquitaine
Louis VII inherited the throne at a young age. In 1137, he married Eleanor of Aquitaine, one of the greatest heiresses in Western Europe. The union brought the vast and wealthy Duchy of Aquitaine under the king's nominal control. However, this advantage turned sour when Louis and Eleanor's marriage collapsed, leading to an annulment in 1152. Eleanor then married Henry Plantagenet, who soon became King Henry II of England. Thus, the southern lands that once belonged to the French crown now fell into the hands of the English monarchy. This event would have dramatic repercussions for centuries, fueling Anglo-French rivalry.

The Second Crusade
Deeply religious, Louis VII took part in the Second Crusade (1147–1149) with other European rulers. The expedition failed to achieve its goals in the Holy Land, and Louis's leadership was criticized. His lengthy absence also allowed some French nobles to assert greater independence.

Conflict with Henry II of England
After Eleanor remarried Henry Plantagenet, Henry inherited Normandy and Anjou, then became Henry II of England in 1154. Together, Henry and Eleanor ruled an "Angevin Empire" that included a large portion of France: Normandy, Anjou, Maine, Touraine, and Aquitaine. Louis VII struggled to contain Henry's growing power, resorting to alliances with other local lords and occasional warfare to maintain a balance.

Royal Prestige and Religious Patronage
Despite these setbacks, Louis VII continued to strengthen ties with the church. He supported the building of Gothic cathedrals, such as the early stages of Notre-Dame in Paris. He also expanded the use of royal justice in the Île-de-France, further establishing the king's role as a defender of order and piety.

---

8. The Roots of Later Centralization

Growing Sense of Kingship
From Hugh Capet through Louis VII, the Capetians emphasized the sacred nature of kingship. They portrayed themselves as protectors of the church and guardians of justice. Over time, this image helped them rally support from townsfolk, clergy, and lesser nobles against larger feudal magnates. Even if a single great lord controlled more land, the king possessed a special, divinely sanctioned status that no other noble could claim.

Succession Practices
A crucial factor in Capetian stability was their consistent ability to produce male heirs. By crowning sons as co-kings, they minimized succession disputes. In contrast, some rival houses experienced inheritance crises or divisions. The Capetians maintained a near-unbroken line, lending predictability and legitimacy to the throne.

Municipal Charters and Economic Base
As commerce grew along the Seine and in other urban centers, the Capetians found a modest but steady source of revenue. By granting communal charters, the king encouraged economic expansion, which in turn increased tax income. This growing financial base, though still small compared to modern standards, gradually enabled the monarchy to fund its own military campaigns without relying solely on feudal levies.

Diplomacy and Church Support
Capetian kings nurtured close relations with the papacy. While disputes over lay investiture and clerical appointments did arise, French kings often acted as protectors of church interests. In return, popes recognized the legitimacy of Capetian rule and occasionally pressured rebellious nobles to submit. This church support was not absolute—popes could also excommunicate or oppose kings—but on balance, it worked in the monarchy's favor compared to many powerful vassals who lacked that aura of divine sanction.

9. Conflict and Cooperation with Neighboring Powers

Flanders, Champagne, and Brittany
Apart from the formidable Anglo-Norman-Angevin realm, French kings also navigated relations with other strong principalities:

- **Flanders**: A wealthy region engaged in North Sea trade. Flanders' counts were sophisticated diplomats, sometimes allied with the English to counter French royal ambitions.
- **Champagne**: Prosperous due to its famous fairs, Champagne's counts held considerable influence and minted their own coins.
- **Brittany**: Culturally distinct with its Celtic heritage, Brittany's dukes or counts tried to maintain autonomy, sometimes allying with English kings.

The Capetians had to juggle these alliances, forging temporary truces, betrothals, and commercial agreements to keep the realm from splintering further.

Holy Roman Empire
To the east lay the German-speaking lands under the Holy Roman Emperor. While the empire's power fluctuated, some emperors meddled in Burgundian or Lotharingian regions. The Capetians generally avoided direct confrontation with the empire, focusing on consolidating their hold in the west. Cross-border noble families often owned lands in both realms, adding another layer of diplomatic complexity.

---

10. Significance of the Early Capetian Era

Foundation for Later Great Kings
Although none of the early Capetian kings matched the territorial reach of their Angevin rivals, they established crucial foundations. Their unwavering dynastic continuity, church alliances, and cautious expansion of royal justice prepared the stage for more decisive kings like Philip II Augustus, Louis VIII, and Louis IX, who would significantly enlarge the royal domain and prestige.

Feudal Monarchs, Not Absolute Rulers
The Capetian rulers from Hugh Capet through Louis VII were essentially feudal monarchs. Their power rested on personal loyalty, feudal contracts, and the

cooperation of powerful vassals. While they bore the title "King of France," their actual day-to-day influence was often confined to the Île-de-France region. Yet, their persistent survival and gradual strengthening of royal authority ensured that, bit by bit, the monarchy became a unifying force in France.

Gradual Development of French Identity
During the 11th and 12th centuries, the French language (in its early medieval form) expanded in literature, courtly culture, and clerical writing. Paris emerged as a cultural hub, especially with the growth of the University of Paris in the early 12th century. Though still overshadowed by powerful principalities, the Capetian court laid the cultural seeds that would bloom in later medieval France.

Shaping the Medieval World
The interplay between kings, nobles, and churchmen in Capetian France was not unique—similar patterns existed in England, the German lands, and elsewhere. However, the Capetian case shows how a dynasty with minimal initial resources could, through steady strategies and advantageous marriages, elevate itself to become the core of a more centralized state. This slow but determined rise of the French monarchy would have major consequences for European politics in the High Middle Ages.

CHAPTER 9: THE HUNDRED YEARS' WAR AND JOAN OF ARC

Introduction

By the early 14th century, the Capetian Dynasty had ruled France for more than three centuries. Gradually, kings like Philip II Augustus, Louis VIII, and Louis IX had expanded royal territory and strengthened central authority. Royal officials called *baillis* and *sénéchaux* enforced laws in newly acquired provinces, and the Crown's financial resources grew through taxes on trade and agriculture. These changes laid the groundwork for a more unified kingdom, even though powerful nobles and cross-Channel ties to England posed constant challenges.

In 1328, the direct Capetian line ended with the death of King Charles IV without a male heir. The French nobility recognized Philip of Valois (Philip VI) as the new king, founding the Valois branch of the Capetian family. Across the Channel, however, England's King Edward III—grandson of the French king Philip IV through his mother—claimed the French throne. This dispute was a key factor igniting the protracted conflict we call the Hundred Years' War (1337–1453). This war would shape France's identity, devastate its countryside, and introduce a new heroine to the national story: Joan of Arc.

In this chapter, we will follow the major phases of the Hundred Years' War. We will see how early English victories rattled French morale, how internal divisions in France exacerbated the crisis, and how Joan of Arc inspired a turning point in the war. Finally, we will explore the eventual recovery of French power under King Charles VII, setting the stage for the Valois consolidation of France in the decades that followed.

1. Background to the Hundred Years' War

The End of the Direct Capetians
The long-reigning Capetian kings had secured an unbroken line of male heirs until

the early 14th century. However, the last direct Capetians—Louis X, Philip V, and Charles IV—died in quick succession without producing surviving sons. Debate raged over succession rights, especially since Charles IV's sister, Isabella, was the mother of King Edward III of England.

A French assembly of nobles invoked an old Frankish principle (later called "Salic Law") that barred inheritance of the crown through the female line. By this logic, the throne passed instead to Philip of Valois, a cousin of the late king. He was crowned Philip VI in 1328. Edward III appeared to accept this at first, doing homage to Philip for his duchy of Aquitaine (in southwestern France), a region that English kings had held or claimed for generations. But the tension between the two monarchs never went away.

Aquitaine and Flanders
Two important regions fueled conflict:

1. **Aquitaine**: A wealthy and fertile area producing wine and other goods. The English Plantagenet kings had inherited Aquitaine through Eleanor of Aquitaine back in the 12th century. Over time, the French kings sought to reduce English power in this region, while the English strove to maintain or expand their holdings.
2. **Flanders**: Dependent on English wool for its cloth industry, Flanders had economic ties to England. Many Flemish townspeople resented French attempts to control them. This made Flanders a flashpoint, as some city leaders looked to England for support against the French Crown.

Edward III's Claim
When relations soured, Edward III renewed his claim to the French crown in 1337. This declaration effectively launched the Hundred Years' War. Initially, it served as a diplomatic and moral pretext for Edward's military actions to protect his possessions in France and build alliances on the Continent.

---

2. The Early Phase

Naval and Diplomatic Moves
The war began with naval skirmishes and alliances. England formed pacts with various rulers in the Low Countries (modern Belgium/Netherlands) and the Holy Roman Empire, hoping to encircle France. Philip VI responded by trying to secure

the loyalty of Flemish towns. Meanwhile, control of the seas mattered for moving troops and supplies; the English scored a key naval victory at the Battle of Sluys (1340), weakening France's ability to launch an invasion across the Channel.

The Battle of Crecy (1346)
One of the most famous early battles was Crecy (in northern France) in 1346. Edward III's army, smaller but better organized, used longbows to devastating effect against the French knights and crossbowmen. The English tactics and discipline outmatched the French chivalric style of charging cavalry, resulting in a major English victory. King Philip VI retreated, and the English went on to capture the strategic port of Calais in 1347, giving them a crucial foothold in northern France.

The Black Death (1347–1351)
In the midst of war, the Black Death arrived in Europe, spreading across France by 1348. This pandemic killed a huge portion of the population—some estimates say up to one-third or more in certain regions. Armies suffered from disease, and agricultural production declined. Both countries paused major offensives for a time, but the social and economic damage was immense. The plague weakened the French Crown's ability to collect taxes and maintain a consistent army, a problem that would haunt future campaigns.

The Battle of Poitiers (1356)
Hostilities resumed in the 1350s, now under the new French king John II (John "the Good"), who succeeded Philip VI. But again, the French suffered a disastrous defeat at the Battle of Poitiers in 1356. The English, led by Edward the Black Prince (Edward III's son), employed tactics similar to Crecy: strategic positioning, disciplined archers, and careful use of defensive terrain. The French cavalry charges failed. King John II himself was captured in battle, an event that shocked the kingdom and plunged it into crisis.

---

3. Civil Strife in France

King John II's Ransom and Tax Burdens
With King John II held prisoner in England, France had to negotiate heavy ransom payments for his release. Meanwhile, the kingdom needed funds for defense. Taxes rose sharply, creating discontent among peasants and urban populations. The

Estates-General, an assembly of nobles, clergy, and commoners, tried to limit royal taxation and gain a say in governance, but their efforts at reform clashed with factions loyal to the Crown.

The Jacquerie (1358)

Resentment over taxes and the war's devastation fueled a major peasant uprising known as the Jacquerie in 1358. Angry peasants in northern France attacked noble estates, blaming the aristocracy for military failures and high taxes. The rebellion was brutally suppressed by noble forces. This violence deepened the divide between peasants and the feudal aristocracy, weakening the kingdom's internal stability.

Charles the Dauphin and the Paris Unrest

While King John II was in captivity, his son Charles (the Dauphin) acted as regent. He faced turmoil in Paris, where a merchant leader, Étienne Marcel, pushed for reforms to constrain royal authority and protect the city from foreign invasion. Marcel and his supporters took control of the city briefly, seeking to ally with the discontented peasants. The situation deteriorated into open conflict; Marcel was eventually killed, and Charles regained control of Paris. But these episodes underscored how vulnerable the monarchy was to internal revolt.

---

4. The Rise of Charles V and Strategic Warfare

Treaty of Brétigny (1360)

In 1360, under immense pressure, France signed the Treaty of Brétigny with England. The treaty set a huge ransom for King John II, ceded extensive lands in southwestern France to the English, and recognized Edward III's expanded holdings. However, Edward temporarily renounced his claim to the French crown. This brought a brief respite from major battles, but it left France smaller and humiliated.

Charles V (1364–1380)

After John II's death (he never fully escaped financial struggles even after partial ransom payments), his son Charles V became king. Nicknamed "the Wise," Charles V reformed the French government and rebuilt the army. He appointed capable generals like Bertrand du Guesclin, who used guerrilla tactics and strategic sieges rather than direct pitched battles. Over time, France recovered some territories lost to England. Du Guesclin's focus on cutting off English supply lines and isolating their garrisons proved effective.

Financial and Administrative Reforms
Charles V understood that to fight a prolonged war, the Crown needed stable finances. He introduced more systematic taxes, including a permanent "taille" (direct tax) on peasants, and improved royal bookkeeping. He also relied on skilled bureaucrats who worked out of Paris. Though some nobles complained about centralization, these measures gradually strengthened the monarchy's hand.

Building Defenses and a Fleet
Charles V invested in fortifications, especially along the northern coast and around key towns. He also began to revive a French navy to counter English shipping. By avoiding large-scale battles and focusing on strategic gains, the French began to chip away at the English position, especially in areas like Normandy and Poitou.

---

5. Renewed Crises

Death of Charles V
When Charles V died in 1380, he left behind a minor heir, Charles VI, only 11 years old. This allowed various royal uncles and princes to take control of the regency. Factional struggles emerged at the French court, especially between the dukes of Burgundy and the dukes of Orléans. Meanwhile, in England, King Richard II faced his own internal difficulties, including the Peasants' Revolt (1381). Both kingdoms temporarily paused their war efforts as they dealt with internal politics.

Charles VI's Madness
Charles VI came of age in 1388, but soon began to exhibit episodes of mental illness, leading him to be called "Charles the Mad." During his bouts of insanity, France effectively lacked a stable monarch. Rival branches of the royal family—primarily the House of Burgundy and the House of Orléans—vied for influence. Their conflict escalated into open civil war, known as the Armagnac-Burgundian feud. This disunity would be disastrous when the English renewed their aggression.

Rise of the Burgundians
The Dukes of Burgundy, controlling territories in eastern France and the Low Countries, became extremely wealthy. They sought to dominate the French court, forging alliances with England to pressure their enemies. On the opposing side, the

Armagnacs (supporters of the Orléans branch) tried to uphold the king's authority but found themselves blocked by Burgundian power.

6. Henry V and the Catastrophe at Agincourt

The Lancastrian Phase
In 1413, Henry V, a dynamic young king, took the English throne. Seeing France paralyzed by internal strife, he renewed the English claim to the French crown and invaded in 1415. This period is often called the Lancastrian phase of the Hundred Years' War (named after Henry V's House of Lancaster).

Battle of Agincourt (1415)
Henry's campaign culminated in the famous Battle of Agincourt. Despite being heavily outnumbered, the English used longbows and defensive positioning to inflict a crushing defeat on the French nobility. Many French knights and nobles were captured or killed. This disaster for France further destabilized the kingdom, as the Burgundians and Armagnacs blamed each other for the defeat instead of uniting against the common enemy.

Treaty of Troyes (1420)
With France collapsing under civil war, the English forced the Treaty of Troyes on King Charles VI. The treaty recognized Henry V as the regent and heir to the French throne, disinheriting Charles VI's own son (the Dauphin, also named Charles). Henry also married Charles VI's daughter, Catherine of Valois, to strengthen his claim. When Henry V and Charles VI both died within a few months of each other (1422), the infant King Henry VI of England was proclaimed King of France according to the treaty. Meanwhile, the Dauphin Charles, disinherited by Troyes, was left controlling only parts of central and southern France.

7. The Rise of Joan of Arc

The Dauphin's Cause
The disinherited Dauphin, sometimes mockingly called the "King of Bourges" (because he held only a small territory around Bourges), refused to recognize the Treaty of Troyes. He still claimed the legitimate right to the crown as Charles VII.

But with the English and their Burgundian allies occupying northern France—including Paris—and with many French nobles unsure of where to place their loyalty, Charles VII struggled to mount a counteroffensive.

A Young Woman's Mission
Amid this grim situation, Joan of Arc, a peasant girl from Domrémy in eastern France, reported visions of saints urging her to support Charles VII. Convinced that she had a divine mandate, she traveled to the Dauphin's court in 1429, persuading his advisers to let her lead an army to relieve the English siege of Orléans. Although skeptical, Charles took a chance, as desperation had set in.

Relief of Orléans (1429)
Against all odds, Joan's arrival transformed French morale. Wearing armor and carrying a banner, she inspired troops and local populations. The French forced the English to lift the siege of Orléans in May 1429—an event widely seen as miraculous. Other swift victories followed, culminating in Joan's insistence that the Dauphin be crowned in the traditional site of Reims Cathedral. In July 1429, Charles was anointed as King Charles VII, a potent symbol that bolstered his legitimacy.

Captivity and Trial
Joan's mission continued, but in 1430 she was captured by Burgundian forces near Compiègne. The Burgundians handed her over to the English, who put her on trial for heresy and other charges. The politically motivated trial ended with her execution by burning at the stake in Rouen in 1431. She was about nineteen years old. While her death was intended to discredit Charles VII, it ultimately made Joan a martyr in the eyes of many French people.

---

8. The Turn of the Tide

Burgundian Reconciliation
After Joan's death, French fortunes did not collapse. Charles VII's government reorganized the army and finances, building on the momentum Joan had sparked. A key turning point came in 1435 with the Treaty of Arras, where the Duke of Burgundy finally broke his alliance with the English and recognized Charles VII as king. This reconciliation restored much of northern France to Charles's side.

Military Reforms
Charles VII introduced reforms to create a more professional army. He established

"compagnies d'ordonnance," permanent troops paid by the Crown, reducing the old reliance on feudal levies that had proven unreliable. Artillery technology advanced during this period, and French gunners became adept at capturing English-held castles and towns.

Reconquest of Normandy and Bordeaux

From the late 1430s onward, the French methodically pushed the English back. Normandy was retaken in the 1440s and 1450s, culminating in the decisive Battle of Formigny (1450). In 1453, the Battle of Castillon near Bordeaux effectively ended English control in southwestern France. The English were left holding only the port city of Calais, which they would keep for another century, but the rest of their vast continental domains were lost.

End of the Hundred Years' War (1453)

With the fall of Bordeaux in 1453, the Hundred Years' War drew to a close. There was no formal peace treaty, but the fighting largely stopped. France emerged battered yet victorious, with Charles VII firmly recognized as king. English ambitions in France shrank drastically, focusing solely on Calais and the Channel Islands. Most of the country now acknowledged the Valois Crown, setting the stage for France's later consolidation.

---

9. Social and Economic Consequences

Agricultural and Population Loss

Repeated invasions, heavy taxation, and shifting battlefronts devastated the countryside, especially in northern France. Farms were ruined, trade routes cut off, and peasants frequently displaced. The population still had not fully recovered from the Black Death, and the war's destruction worsened matters. In many districts, entire villages were abandoned.

Growth of National Feeling

The war also fostered an early sense of "French" identity. Royal propaganda, combined with Joan of Arc's martyrdom, helped people in different provinces see themselves as part of a shared cause. This sentiment did not erase local loyalties—regional identities remained strong—but the idea of a French kingdom led by a divinely sanctioned king gained wider acceptance.

Changing Warfare and Technology
During the Hundred Years' War, new military technologies emerged or developed further, such as the longbow, improved plate armor, and more effective cannons. Siege tactics evolved, and the role of permanent armies expanded. By the end of the war, the French monarchy had a stronger, more centralized approach to military organization than it had in the early days of feudal levies.

Noble Power and Monarchy
Many high-ranking nobles died in battles like Crecy, Poitiers, and Agincourt. This loss, coupled with the Crown's wartime necessity to tax and maintain troops, gradually shifted power from the nobility to the monarchy. Kings learned they could bypass feudal obligations by collecting direct taxes and funding professional armies, reducing their dependence on barons who might rebel or side with foreign enemies.

---

10. Joan of Arc's Legacy and the Path Forward

Posthumous Rehabilitation
In 1456, a second church trial cleared Joan of Arc's name of heresy, reaffirming her as an innocent victim. Her story endured through the centuries, symbolizing French resistance and divine favor. Although she would not be canonized until the early 20th century, Joan's heroism and sacrifice became an integral part of France's national narrative.

The Ascendancy of Charles VII
After 1453, Charles VII capitalized on the monarchy's wartime innovations. He extended royal justice and built a more stable financial system, including taxes like the *taille* and the *gabelle* (a salt tax). The king's advisers worked to curb feudal privileges, marking a major step in France's centralization. Charles VII's success laid foundations for later Valois monarchs, who continued to unify the realm.

Entering a New Era
By the mid-15th century, the Hundred Years' War ended, and the kingdom slowly recovered. France was on the cusp of major transitions. As commerce revived, Renaissance ideas would soon filter in from Italy. The monarchy, having survived its greatest test against England, would focus on strengthening control over its own nobles and territories.

Historical Significance

The Hundred Years' War was a defining conflict for medieval France, reshaping its political structures, military organization, and collective identity. Joan of Arc emerged as a national heroine who rallied the French when all seemed lost. Her role was both military and symbolic, inspiring future generations to see the French Crown as the embodiment of their shared destiny. In the next chapter, we will examine how the Valois dynasty continued to consolidate power in the aftermath of the war, leading France toward a more unified and robust state.

Conclusion

The Hundred Years' War tested the very survival of the French monarchy. Weaknesses in the feudal system, civil strife, and superior English tactics allowed England to dominate much of northern France for decades. Internal divisions—especially between the Burgundian and Armagnac factions—nearly destroyed any chance of the Crown defending its lands.

Yet from this desperate situation, a remarkable turnaround occurred. Joan of Arc's intervention at Orléans and Reims revitalized the French cause, while Charles VII's reforms ultimately reclaimed nearly all of France. The war's end in 1453 ushered in a new confidence for the Valois kings. Though the land lay in ruins in many places, the seeds of a centralized and stronger French monarchy were planted.

We now move to **Chapter 10**, where we will explore how the Valois dynasty built on the victory in the Hundred Years' War, overcame noble opposition, and laid the groundwork for the French Renaissance and the modern concept of a unified nation-state.

CHAPTER 10: THE RISE OF THE VALOIS AND THE CONSOLIDATION OF POWER

Introduction

The conclusion of the Hundred Years' War in 1453 left France under the rule of King Charles VII, a monarch who had proven his ability to restore the kingdom's fortunes. Yet, France still faced significant challenges. The war had ravaged the countryside, the treasury needed replenishing, and powerful nobles continued to guard their privileges.

Over the next few decades, the Valois kings—beginning with Charles VII and continuing through Louis XI, Charles VIII, and Louis XII—strengthened the monarchy and expanded royal authority over regions that had functioned almost independently. This era saw the growth of a more professional bureaucracy, the forging of alliances through diplomatic marriages, and the assertion of control over once-autonomous duchies like Brittany.

In this chapter, we will examine how the Valois rulers consolidated their power, subdued rebellious nobles, and laid a path toward modern statehood. We will also see the seeds of the French Renaissance and the kingdom's increasing engagement with Italian politics. By the early 16th century, France stood as one of Europe's foremost powers, setting the stage for the reign of Francis I and the vibrant cultural transformation that followed.

1. Charles VII

Restoring the Monarchy
Following the end of the Hundred Years' War, Charles VII focused on rebuilding the kingdom's foundations. Having survived the war's darkest days, he carried the

reputation of "Charles the Victorious." However, his success depended on the reforms he enacted to centralize power:

1. **Standing Army**: Charles continued developing permanent, paid companies of men-at-arms (*compagnies d'ordonnance*). This force was loyal to the Crown rather than to individual nobles, a major shift from feudal levies.
2. **Financial and Tax Reforms**: He improved collection of the *taille* (direct tax) and introduced new levies like the *gabelle* (salt tax). These provided a steadier income, allowing the king to maintain the standing army and sponsor reconstruction projects.
3. **Royal Administration**: Charles refined the roles of royal officers—*baillis*, *sénéchaux*, and a network of inspectors—who enforced royal justice. He aimed to reduce the arbitrary power of local lords.

Relations with Nobles

Many nobles had fought either with or against the king during the war. Charles used a mix of diplomacy and force to keep them in check. He rewarded loyal families with titles and lands, while those suspected of treason were stripped of powers. Over time, fewer nobles could challenge the king's growing authority.

The Pragmatic Sanction of Bourges (1438)

This decree reasserted the Crown's control over appointments of high church officials in France. While it respected the authority of the pope, it curtailed papal influence in French ecclesiastical affairs. This reinforced the concept of "Gallicanism," the idea that the French church had certain independent rights under royal protection.

Legacy

By the time Charles VII died in 1461, France was still healing, but its monarchy was far stronger than at any point during the war. He had proven that a determined king—backed by a professional army and stable finances—could outmaneuver rival lords.

---

2. Louis XI

A Shrewd Ruler

Louis XI, Charles VII's son, earned the nickname "the Universal Spider" for his intricate webs of diplomacy, espionage, and cunning. He focused on breaking the power of overmighty nobles, especially Charles the Bold, Duke of Burgundy, who commanded vast territories stretching from the Low Countries to eastern France. Louis XI excelled at pitting his enemies against each other and using marriage alliances to undermine ducal power.

Conflict with Burgundy

The Duchy of Burgundy under Charles the Bold was almost a separate state. Charles dreamed of forging a "middle kingdom" between France and the Holy Roman Empire. Fearing an independent Burgundy, Louis XI worked tirelessly to thwart Charles's ambitions:

1. **Alliances with Swiss Cantons**: Louis supported the Swiss against Charles the Bold, knowing the Swiss infantry could challenge Burgundy's cavalry.
2. **Diplomatic Maneuvers**: He negotiated truces, double-crossed allies, and used ransoms or secret treaties to keep Charles off balance.

The Fall of Charles the Bold (1477)

Charles the Bold died in battle against the Swiss at Nancy in 1477. His lands were left without a strong male heir. Louis XI quickly moved to seize Burgundy (the French duchy itself), Picardy, and other territories, arguing that they were fiefs of the French Crown that reverted to the king upon the duke's death. Meanwhile, Charles's daughter, Mary of Burgundy, married Maximilian of Habsburg, ensuring that parts of the Burgundian inheritance (in the Low Countries) went to the Habsburgs.

Centralization and Economic Growth

With Burgundy largely subdued, Louis XI consolidated the royal domain. He fostered trade fairs, improved roads, and encouraged commerce in towns. By negotiating commercial treaties, he integrated the kingdom into broader European networks. This economic development bolstered royal tax revenues, further freeing the Crown from dependence on feudal levies.

Legacy of Louis XI

Known for his cunning and sometimes ruthless methods, Louis XI firmly established the principle that the monarchy could—and should—bring powerful duchies under centralized control. He left behind a more unified France, with many key provinces securely under the king's hand. While his style was not always popular, his achievements in uniting large parts of the kingdom were undeniable.

3. Charles VIII and the Italian Venture

Regency and Brittany
Charles VIII was only 13 when Louis XI died, so a regency was needed. His elder sister, Anne of France (also called Anne of Beaujeu), acted as regent. One major challenge was the future of Brittany, an almost independent duchy. Duke Francis II of Brittany sought to keep his lands out of French hands, but the regent maneuvered diplomatically to secure Brittany through marriage.

Marriage to Anne of Brittany (1491)
When Duke Francis II died, his daughter Anne of Brittany became duchess. Seeking foreign support, she was briefly betrothed to Maximilian of Habsburg. However, French forces intervened. Under political pressure, Anne of Brittany married King Charles VIII in 1491, effectively bringing Brittany into the French royal domain. Though she maintained some independent rights as duchess, Brittany was now closely tied to the Crown—a significant step in territorial unification.

The Italian Wars Begin
Eager to claim the Kingdom of Naples, Charles VIII launched an invasion of Italy in 1494. He believed he had dynastic rights through the Angevin line. French armies, equipped with modern artillery, quickly overran parts of the Italian peninsula. Yet they faced fierce resistance from a coalition of Italian states, Spain, the Holy Roman Empire, and the papacy, alarmed by French aggression. This first foray marked the start of the long Italian Wars (1494–1559).

Consequences at Home
Charles's Italian expedition was initially triumphant but ultimately drained the treasury and overstretched French forces. Although it brought new cultural influences back to France—Italian Renaissance art and ideas—it also embroiled the kingdom in costly foreign entanglements. Charles VIII died in 1498 without surviving sons, leaving the throne to his cousin Louis of Orléans, who became Louis XII.

---

4. Louis XII and Further Italian Ambitions

A Popular King
Louis XII, known as the "Father of the People," reduced some taxes and tried to

reconcile with domestic factions. He annulled his previous marriage to wed Anne of Brittany, thus retaining Brittany's connection to the Crown. Generally well-liked by his subjects, Louis XII continued the monarchy's centralizing policies but aimed to rule with a more conciliatory tone than Louis XI.

Italian Campaigns
Louis XII pursued claims in Milan (through his grandmother Valentina Visconti) and Naples. His armies succeeded in taking Milan in 1499, but holding onto both Milan and Naples proved difficult. Spain, under Ferdinand of Aragon, contested Naples, and shifting alliances in Italy produced frequent wars and treaties.

Administration Reforms
Building on earlier innovations, Louis XII employed royal councils to oversee finances, justice, and military organization. He also sought the advice of notable jurists and humanists, reflecting the growing influence of Renaissance thought in French governance. Town charters expanded, encouraging economic activity, though wars remained a heavy financial burden.

Legal Codification
Louis XII sponsored efforts to codify customary laws in different regions of France, aiming to standardize legal practices under royal oversight. While local "coutumes" still varied, the Crown's push for uniformity was a step toward modern legal centralization. The king also emphasized the importance of trained judges and administrators, many of whom were educated in newly established or reformed universities.

End of Reign and Succession
By the time Louis XII died in 1515, France was a stronger kingdom than it had been during the Hundred Years' War, yet still entangled in Italian conflicts. He left no male heir, so the crown passed to his young cousin Francis of Angoulême, who became King Francis I. With this transition, the Valois line continued, but now poised to embrace the full flourishing of the Renaissance era in France.

---

5. Unifying the Realm

Expanding the Royal Domain
From Charles VII through Louis XII, the Crown systematically absorbed or tamed major feudal lordships—Burgundy, Brittany, Anjou, Maine, Provence (through

inheritance), and others. By the early 16th century, the "kingdom of France" was more geographically coherent than ever before, though there were still enclaves, like Navarre in the southwest, not fully integrated.

Provincial Governors and Royal Officers

To manage these enlarged territories, the kings appointed governors and royal officials who enforced royal decrees, collected taxes, and oversaw local courts. The *Parlements* (provincial high courts), most famously the Parlement of Paris, interpreted and registered royal edicts. Over time, these bodies became key pillars of royal authority, though they also defended local privileges, creating friction with the monarchy.

Military Evolution

The monarchy's standing army, begun under Charles VII, evolved further. Kings now had access to professional Swiss or German mercenaries in addition to French troops. The nobility gradually shifted from feudal cavalry duties to roles in the royal army or local governance. Artillery units played a growing role, reflecting lessons learned in the Hundred Years' War and the Italian campaigns.

Ties with the Church

Relations between the French Crown and the papacy fluctuated, especially with French involvement in Italy. Yet the idea of a "Gallican Church"—one loyal to Rome in doctrine but with significant autonomy under the king—continued to solidify. The French monarchy controlled episcopal appointments, ensuring that high church offices often went to nobles or clients loyal to the Crown.

---

6. Socioeconomic Changes and the Dawn of the French Renaissance

Population and Towns

After the devastation of the Hundred Years' War, France's population gradually rebounded. Towns and cities expanded trade networks, aided by improved roads and the relative stability brought by strong monarchs. Guilds regulated crafts, while merchant families grew in wealth and influence.

Early Renaissance Influences

French nobles and kings were fascinated by Italian art and scholarship. Charles

VIII's Italian expedition had exposed them to Renaissance architecture, painting, and humanist ideas. Under Louis XII and into the reign of Francis I, Italian artists and architects like Leonardo da Vinci were invited to France. Castles like those in the Loire Valley (e.g., Amboise, Blois) began to incorporate Renaissance elements, blending French Gothic with Italian styles.

Printing and Education
The printing press, introduced to France in the late 15th century, spurred literacy among elites and the middle classes. Universities evolved, and new colleges arose, sometimes guided by humanist curricula. Greek and Latin classics, along with religious works, circulated more widely. Though literacy rates for commoners remained low, the spread of ideas among educated circles foreshadowed deeper cultural transformations.

Social Stratification
Despite economic growth, the gap between rich and poor remained wide. Nobles retained privileges, while peasants often struggled with taxes and feudal dues. However, the Crown's centralization weakened the power of local barons, leading some peasants and townspeople to see the king as a protector against abusive local lords. This perception helped bolster royal prestige.

---

7. Diplomacy and Marriage Alliances

Habsburg Rivalries
France's expansion clashed with the ambitions of the Habsburg dynasty, which controlled Austria, the Holy Roman Empire, and, by inheritance from Burgundy, the Low Countries. Through marriage, the Habsburgs also acquired Spain (when Joanna of Castile married Philip the Handsome, son of Maximilian of Austria and Mary of Burgundy). This created an enormous "Habsburg ring" around France. The Valois kings sought to counter this encirclement through alliances with England, various Italian states, and sometimes the Ottoman Empire, in a diplomatic dance that would intensify under Francis I.

Royal Marriages
Marriages arranged by the French Crown served to secure or pacify neighboring territories. We saw this with Anne of Brittany's union first to Charles VIII and then to Louis XII, tying Brittany to the Crown. Similarly, the monarchy placed daughters

or sisters in noble courts abroad to influence foreign policy. While not always successful, these marriages gave the French kings a chance to negotiate peace treaties or secure claims to contested lands.

---

8. Noble Resistance and the Last Feudal Revolts

Regional Power-Brokers
Even as the monarchy grew stronger, certain nobles still possessed considerable autonomy. The Bourbon family, for example, was granted wide lands. Occasional revolts flared when nobles felt threatened by new taxes, central directives, or monarchical interference with their ancestral rights.

The "Ligue du Bien Public" (1465)
During Louis XI's reign, a coalition of great lords formed the "League of the Public Weal," claiming they wanted to defend public welfare against the king's heavy-handed policies. In reality, they aimed to preserve their feudal independence. Although Louis XI had to make concessions, he eventually wore down the coalition. This pattern—noble alliances rebelling against strong kings—continued sporadically into the 16th century, though each revolt was less effective as the monarchy consolidated.

Court Culture
As direct military resistance to the king became riskier, nobles often channeled their ambitions into court life. Serving the king as courtiers, royal councilors, or military officers brought prestige and wealth. The royal court in Paris or in the Loire Valley became a center of patronage where personal influence could outweigh feudal claims. This social shift from local power bases to the royal court further enhanced the Crown's authority.

---

9. Preparing for a New Era

Louis XII's Final Years
Despite ongoing Italian campaigns, Louis XII managed to keep France relatively stable. He continued efforts to reduce conflict among nobles and strengthen ties

with urban centers. However, the Italian Wars remained inconclusive, draining resources and leading to shifting alliances.

Succession of Francis I (1515)
When Louis XII died without a male heir, the crown passed to Francis of Angoulême. This new king, crowned as Francis I, inherited a France that was more unified, better administered, and open to Renaissance influences from Italy. Francis I would fully embrace these cultural developments, inviting Italian artists and scholars to his court and championing humanist education.

Looking Ahead
France in the early 16th century had come a long way from the devastation of the Hundred Years' War. The kingdom was still feudal in many respects, but the monarchy now had the administrative structures, financial base, and military capacity to exert real power over most of its territory. The Valois kings had subdued or absorbed once-independent duchies and baronies, reduced internal revolts, and set the stage for a blossoming of arts and learning.

Yet challenges loomed. The rivalry with the Habsburgs, including Charles V (who in 1519 would become Holy Roman Emperor and already held Spain, Austria, and the Netherlands), would spark repeated conflicts. Domestically, religious tensions began to surface, foreshadowing the Reformation's impact in the decades ahead. The monarchy's continued quest for glory in Italy would also persist, leading to both triumphs and setbacks.

---

10. Significance of the Valois Consolidation

Foundations of the Modern State
From Charles VII's recovery after the Hundred Years' War to Louis XII's steady governance, the Valois kings laid lasting structures for governance. They showed that a monarch with a permanent army and a steady stream of tax revenue could overcome feudal fragmentation. Their network of royal officers and courts further ingrained the idea that ultimate authority rested with the Crown, not local barons.

Unity Through Territory and Administration
The absorption of Brittany and control of Burgundy meant that key regions once semi-independent were brought directly under royal influence. This advanced the idea of a single realm called "France," though linguistic and cultural diversity still

thrived. A more uniform administration gave the Crown tools to impose laws and collect taxes consistently.

Diplomatic Reach and Cultural Exchange
Valois kings engaged in broader European diplomacy, forging marriages and alliances that connected them to Spain, Austria, and Italy. Though the wars in Italy were costly, they also introduced French elites to Renaissance art, architecture, and scholarship. This cultural cross-pollination enriched the kingdom, making France a rising center of learning and artistic expression.

Preparing the Ground for the Renaissance
As the monarchy grew in confidence, it patronized scholars, artists, and architects, laying the groundwork for a distinctively French Renaissance under Francis I and his successors. The court's patronage of humanism and the arts would soon elevate France as a European cultural leader.

Conclusion

By the early 16th century, the Valois dynasty had transformed France from a patchwork of feudal principalities into a more centralized kingdom. After the Hundred Years' War, kings like Charles VII, Louis XI, Charles VIII, and Louis XII systematically subdued powerful nobles, annexed strategic territories, and improved royal institutions. Military reforms and new tax structures gave the Crown the tools to maintain authority. Diplomatic marriages and engagements in Italy expanded France's influence—though they also embroiled the kingdom in ongoing continental conflicts.

As we move into the next phase, **Chapter 11** will detail how the French Renaissance unfolded under Francis I. It will also explore the evolving role of the monarchy in fostering the arts and the rise of new intellectual movements. This era saw both the crowning achievements of Valois patronage and the emergence of deeper religious tensions that would soon erupt into the Wars of Religion.

CHAPTER 11: THE FRENCH RENAISSANCE UNDER FRANCIS I

Introduction

By the early 16th century, France was emerging from the long shadow of the Hundred Years' War. Under the later Valois kings—Charles VII, Louis XI, Charles VIII, and Louis XII—the monarchy had grown more centralized, absorbing key territories and building a more cohesive administrative system. When King Louis XII died in 1515 without a surviving son, the crown passed to his young cousin, Francis of Angoulême, who became **Francis I**. With this succession, the Valois dynasty continued, but now a new era was dawning.

Francis I embodied the ideals of the **Renaissance**: he was charismatic, fascinated by humanist scholarship, and enthusiastic about arts and architecture. His reign (1515–1547) introduced a flourishing of culture in France, influenced heavily by Italian models. The king's military ambitions, especially in Italy, also shaped diplomacy and warfare. Rivalry with the Habsburg Emperor Charles V (who controlled vast domains encircling France) defined much of Francis's foreign policy.

This chapter explores the major dimensions of the French Renaissance under Francis I, including artistic patronage, the spread of humanism, religious reform currents, political maneuvers, and the socioeconomic shifts that accompanied these developments. By examining these facets, we will see how Francis's reign laid enduring foundations for the cultural and political identity of early modern France.

1. The Accession of Francis I and Initial Challenges

Bloodline and Marriage
Francis I was the son of Charles, Count of Angoulême, and Louise of Savoy, making him a cousin of Louis XII. Although not a direct descendant of Louis XII in the male line, he was next in line under Salic Law. Louis XII sought to maintain a smooth transition by marrying Francis to his daughter, Claude of France, securing the

Valois lineage and keeping the province of Brittany (which Claude had inherited from her mother, Anne of Brittany) within the royal domain.

When Francis ascended the throne at age 20, he inherited a kingdom largely at peace. However, tension with the Habsburgs and continuing claims in Italy promised new conflicts. Domestically, he stepped into a more centralized administrative framework that his predecessors had built—permanent taxes like the *taille* and the *gabelle*, a standing army, and improved royal councils. Yet, Francis had his own vision for kingship, focusing on glory through cultural patronage and martial prowess.

The Battle of Marignano (1515)
Eager to revive French claims in northern Italy (particularly the Duchy of Milan), Francis launched a campaign soon after his coronation. His decisive victory at the **Battle of Marignano** (1515) near Milan established him as a formidable military leader. Employing Swiss mercenaries, artillery, and French cavalry, Francis overcame the Swiss forces allied with the Milanese. This triumph gave France control over Milan, reinforcing Francis's sense of destiny as a Renaissance prince.

However, consolidating Milan proved challenging. Italian states, the Pope, and the emerging Spanish-Habsburg power under Charles V contested French dominance. Still, Marignano boosted Francis's popularity at home and signaled the beginning of a reign that would mix warfare with the pursuit of cultural magnificence.

Coronation and Court Pageantry
Francis's coronation at Reims in 1515 was an extravagant affair, reflecting the new king's taste for splendor. Tournaments, banquets, and displays of heraldry enhanced his chivalric image. Many knights and nobles rallied around him, hoping for patronage. The court at Blois and later at Fontainebleau grew in opulence, showcasing tapestries, sculptures, and architectural innovations influenced by Italian artists. This emphasis on court culture became a hallmark of Francis's rule, setting the stage for widespread artistic renewal.

---

2. Art and Architecture

Italian Influences
Francis I admired Italian Renaissance masters and invited many of them to his court. The most famous figure to arrive was **Leonardo da Vinci**, who came to

France around 1516. Though aging, Leonardo brought with him the Mona Lisa and other works, as well as his notebooks filled with engineering and anatomical studies. The king lodged him at the manor of Clos Lucé near the royal château of Amboise, providing a pension and honor. Leonardo's influence, while subtle, gave impetus to French artists and architects to look more closely at Italian styles of perspective, realism, and classical motifs.

Other Italian artists, such as **Rosso Fiorentino** and **Francesco Primaticcio**, later joined the royal court, decorating the newly transformed **Château de Fontainebleau**. These court painters and decorators shaped what came to be called the **Fontainebleau School**, characterized by mannerist elegance and refined ornamentation. The result was a fusion of Italian Renaissance aesthetics with French Gothic traditions, seen in elaborately carved interiors, frescoed galleries, and formal gardens.

Royal Building Projects
Under Francis I, significant construction and renovation projects took place:

1. **Château de Fontainebleau**: Expanded from an old royal hunting lodge into a grand palace, showcasing Italian-inspired galleries (like the Gallery of Francis I) adorned with frescoes and stucco figures.
2. **Château de Chambord**: Begun in 1519 in the Loire Valley, Chambord remains one of the most iconic examples of French Renaissance architecture. It features a distinctive double-helix staircase (often attributed to ideas from Leonardo da Vinci), classical pilasters, and a roofline bristling with decorative spires.
3. **Louvre Improvements**: In Paris, Francis started modernizing the medieval Louvre fortress, converting it into a royal residence with more comfortable living quarters and elegant façades.

The king's building ambitions symbolized royal grandeur, while also supporting a network of sculptors, painters, engineers, and craftsmen who gained employment and inspiration from these lavish projects.

Court Culture and Festivals
Francis I's court became a microcosm of Renaissance life, with noble courtiers competing in jousts, pageants, and creative performances. Poets, musicians, and philosophers found patronage, producing works that celebrated the king's virtues. Lavish court festivals often combined political objectives with cultural display. When Francis entertained foreign diplomats, he used these spectacles to exhibit

French sophistication and might, hoping to secure alliances or intimidate potential rivals.

---

3. The Spread of Humanism and Learning

Humanist Circles
The Renaissance's defining intellectual movement, **humanism**, emphasized the study of classical texts (Latin and Greek), the pursuit of eloquence, and the shaping of morally upright citizens. Under Francis I, humanist thinkers like **Guillaume Budé** gained royal favor. Budé was a leading scholar of Greek who advised the king on educational reforms, library acquisitions, and cultural policy.

The king supported the creation of the **Collège Royal** in Paris (later known as the Collège de France), an institution where professors could teach Greek, Hebrew, and other subjects free from the strict scholastic curriculum of the University of Paris. This step signaled a growing openness to new learning. Francis also assembled libraries of manuscripts and printed books, encouraging the growth of **printing presses** in cities like Paris and Lyon.

Printing Press and Literacy
Although literacy rates among commoners remained low, printed books significantly increased the circulation of ideas among the nobility, clergy, and urban middle classes. By the early 16th century, Paris was a bustling center of the book trade. Lyon became another major hub due to its trade fairs and proximity to Italy.

Humanist books on grammar, philosophy, history, and theology proliferated. Writers such as **François Rabelais** produced satirical works—*Pantagruel* and *Gargantua*—that critiqued societal norms and championed humanist education. While often bawdy and irreverent, Rabelais's works reflected the intellectual ferment of the era. The monarchy, for the most part, tolerated these writings, so long as they did not overtly challenge the king's authority or the fundamental doctrines of the Catholic Church.

Women and Intellectual Life
Noblewomen like **Marguerite de Navarre** (Francis's sister) hosted salons where poets, theologians, and philosophers gathered. Marguerite herself wrote poems and religious meditations, demonstrating the increased—though still limited—participation of aristocratic women in literary circles. While formal

education for women remained rare, these gatherings allowed them some voice in cultural debate. Marguerite's patronage also protected certain reform-minded writers, as we shall see in the context of early religious controversies.

---

4. Concordat of Bologna and Relations with the Church

Negotiations with the Papacy
In 1516, Francis I concluded the **Concordat of Bologna** with Pope Leo X. This agreement replaced the earlier Pragmatic Sanction of Bourges and granted the French king extensive authority over church appointments in his realm. Francis gained the right to nominate bishops and abbots, subject to papal confirmation. This arrangement strengthened royal control over ecclesiastical revenues and personnel while still recognizing the pope's spiritual primacy.

For the papacy, the concordat ended the more stringent provisions of the Pragmatic Sanction, which had limited Rome's influence in France. In return, the pope secured a reliable flow of annates (payments for appointments). The Concordat of Bologna thus institutionalized a **Gallican** (French-centric) church structure that balanced royal prerogatives with papal authority.

Impact on French Governance
Having the power to appoint high church officials allowed Francis to reward loyal nobles or educated clerics with bishoprics and abbeys. This integrated the Church more closely into the state apparatus. Church lands, though still outside direct royal taxation, often contributed to the Crown's finances through negotiated aids. The monarchy's hand in ecclesiastical affairs also meant fewer open conflicts with the papacy, although tension lingered if French foreign policy clashed with Rome's interests in Italy.

Popular Reactions
Most ordinary believers were likely unaware of the legal intricacies behind this concordat. They continued to practice Catholicism in local parishes largely unaffected by the higher-level appointments. However, some reform-minded intellectuals and clerics saw the king's expanded patronage as an opportunity for quiet religious renewal, while conservative voices feared royal domination could corrupt the spiritual mission of the Church.

5. Diplomacy and Warfare

Rise of the Habsburg Empire
In 1519, Charles of Habsburg inherited a vast collection of territories: Spain (including its growing American empire), Austria, the Low Countries, and southern Italy. Elected as the Holy Roman Emperor, he became **Charles V**, effectively surrounding France with Habsburg lands. For Francis I, this posed an existential challenge, as he saw the Habsburgs' encirclement as a threat to French independence and territorial ambitions in Italy.

Italian Wars Continue
From the 1520s onward, Francis engaged in repeated conflicts with Charles V over Milan and other Italian states. Battles seesawed. Notably:

- **Battle of Pavia (1525)**: A catastrophic defeat for Francis. Captured by imperial forces, the king was forced to sign the **Treaty of Madrid (1526)**, relinquishing claims in Italy and Burgundy to secure his release. Upon regaining freedom, Francis repudiated the agreement, claiming it was made under duress.
- Alliances with the Ottoman Empire: In a bid to curb Habsburg power, Francis courted the Ottoman sultan, Suleiman the Magnificent, an unconventional partnership that scandalized many Christian rulers but provided a strategic counterweight to Charles V.

Treaties and Shifting Alliances
Diplomatic realignments marked Francis's reign. The **League of Cognac (1526)** united France with the Papal States, Florence, Milan, and Venice against the emperor. French arms marched again in Lombardy, sometimes gaining, sometimes losing territory. By the 1530s, neither side achieved a decisive victory, leading to temporary truces. Francis occasionally tried negotiations with Charles V to arrange marriages or mutual non-aggression pacts, but deep distrust persisted.

Burgundy and the Low Countries
Charles V claimed the former Duchy of Burgundy, which Louis XI had integrated into France decades earlier. Francis refused to cede it, insisting it was a rightful part of the royal domain. Meanwhile, commercial ties between France and the Low Countries—now Habsburg possessions—complicated the rivalry, as merchants wanted peace to facilitate trade. Repeated border skirmishes and economic sanctions flared. Ultimately, Francis never relinquished Burgundy, though it took extensive resources to defend it against Habsburg claims.

6. Religious Reforms and the Early Roots of Protestantism

Luther's Ideas Reach France
While Francis I was personally Catholic, his kingdom was not immune to the **Protestant Reformation** that began in the German states under Martin Luther (1517 onward). Translations of the Bible and Protestant tracts circulated secretly through France's growing network of printers. Reform-minded French clerics and scholars studied Luther's works, discussing the possibility of curbing church abuses and emphasizing salvation by faith.

Marguerite de Navarre and Protecting Reformers
Within the royal circle, **Marguerite de Navarre**—the king's sister—harbored sympathy for religious reform. She corresponded with prominent thinkers and shielded some from persecution. The king himself displayed a degree of initial tolerance, hoping that moderate reforms might strengthen the church in France without provoking full-scale heresy. However, radical preaching or direct attacks on the king's authority were not tolerated.

Affair of the Placards (1534)
A turning point came in 1534 with the so-called **Affair of the Placards**: anti-Catholic posters appeared overnight in Paris and several provincial cities, even on the door of the king's bedchamber. Outraged by this blatant disrespect, Francis I adopted harsher measures against suspected Protestants. Public burnings of heretics increased, and censorship tightened. The incident soured Francis's view of religious dissidents, shifting him toward a policy of repression.

John Calvin's Flight
Among those compelled to leave France was **John Calvin**, a French theologian who settled in Basel and later in Geneva. His *Institutes of the Christian Religion* (1536) laid the foundations of Calvinism. Though not yet a massive movement in France, these early seeds of Protestantism would eventually flower into the Huguenot communities, leading to the Wars of Religion after Francis's death. For the moment, Francis retained control, balancing alliances with Catholic powers abroad and enforcing a moderate-to-strict Catholic conformity at home.

7. Socioeconomic Shifts and the Changing Social Hierarchy

Urban Growth and Commerce
Amid wars and religious tensions, the French economy showed signs of recovery from the disruptions of the previous century. Towns like Lyon, Rouen, and Bordeaux grew as centers of trade. The fairs of Lyon attracted merchants from across Europe, dealing in textiles, metals, and spices. Banking houses expanded, offering credit and exchange services, while maritime trade grew, with vessels from Normandy and Brittany venturing to Atlantic routes.

Agriculture and Land Ownership
Most of the population remained rural, working as peasants or tenant farmers on noble or ecclesiastical estates. While agricultural methods were still rudimentary, the reduced population (due to earlier plagues and wars) meant land could be more plentiful in some areas. Some peasants gained better tenancy arrangements, though feudal dues persisted. The Crown's taxation—especially the *taille*—weighed heavily on peasant communities, funding wars in Italy and lavish royal patronage.

Nobility and Titles
Francis I's reign saw the continued evolution of the nobility. Many noble families advanced at court, seeking royal appointments as governors, military officers, or ambassadors. Acquiring an office, like a judgeship in a *Parlement*, could confer nobility (*noblesse de robe*), expanding the aristocracy beyond feudal lords (*noblesse d'épée*). This shift from purely feudal identity toward service-based nobility enriched the monarchy, as offices could be sold or used as rewards.

Legal Centralization
Building on the legacy of Charles VII and Louis XI, Francis I further promoted the codification of local customs, turning them into standardized law codes recognized by royal courts. This move curtailed arbitrary noble justice in rural areas. While local differences in law remained, the monarchy strove to unify them under centralized oversight. These legal reforms contributed to a sense of national cohesion, even if enforcement varied by region.

8. Literary and Intellectual Achievements

Poets and Writers
The French Renaissance produced a wave of literary talent, much of it supported by the Crown or by wealthy patrons. Notable figures include:

- **Clément Marot**: A court poet who wrote verses that blended elegance and wit, though he occasionally ran afoul of religious authorities.
- **François Rabelais**: Mentioned earlier, best known for his satires *Gargantua* and *Pantagruel*, which critiqued scholasticism and championed humanistic learning.
- **Marguerite de Navarre**: Authored *Heptaméron*, a collection of tales drawing from Boccaccio's influence and her personal reflections on religion and society.

Growth of French as a Literary Language
Though Latin remained the scholarly lingua franca, Francis I encouraged the use of **French** in official documents. The Ordinance of Villers-Cotterêts (1539) mandated that judicial and administrative acts be recorded in French rather than Latin, promoting a clearer national identity and accessibility. Over time, French evolved as a refined literary language, used in poetry, prose, and courtly discourse.

Humanist Philosophers
Influenced by Erasmus and other European thinkers, French humanists debated moral philosophy, theology, and the role of classical wisdom in contemporary society. Groups of educated clerics, lawyers, and scholars met in private circles to discuss translations of Plato or commentaries on the Church Fathers. While most avoided direct challenges to official Catholic doctrine, they advocated for pious reforms, the education of the laity, and the uplifting of moral standards among the clergy.

---

9. The Late Reign of Francis I

Renewed Wars with Charles V
In the 1540s, Francis resumed war against the Habsburgs, seeking to recover territories lost after Pavia and to secure alliances with Protestant German princes. Despite some successes, these campaigns did not yield decisive gains. By the

mid-1540s, both Francis and Charles V were exhausted by conflict, leading to a tenuous truce.

Increasing Religious Persecution

The monarchy's stance on heresy hardened over time. Francis I established the **Chambre Ardente** ("Burning Chamber") within the Parlement of Paris to judge heretics. Public executions were intended to deter the spread of Protestant ideas. Nonetheless, clandestine Protestant congregations formed, especially in urban centers. While still small, these communities foreshadowed the turmoil of future religious wars.

Illness and Death (1547)

Francis grew ill in his later years, suffering from various ailments possibly related to the rigors of war and the stresses of governance. He died in 1547 at the Château de Rambouillet. Despite occasional setbacks—such as the defeat at Pavia and the ongoing Habsburg threat—Francis I left a kingdom that was more culturally vibrant and administratively organized than it had been at his accession. His patronage of the arts and humanist learning earned him a lasting reputation as the father of the French Renaissance.

---

10. Conclusion

The reign of Francis I marked a watershed in French history. Emerging from the Middle Ages into the Renaissance, France under Francis combined ambitious artistic patronage, intellectual ferment, centralized governance, and formidable (if costly) military ventures. Italian influences permeated court life, architecture, and scholarship, giving birth to a distinctly French interpretation of the Renaissance style. Meanwhile, humanist learning thrived through the Collège Royal and the spread of printing presses, laying intellectual groundwork that would endure for centuries.

Yet Francis I also presided over the first stirrings of religious conflict. His early tolerance for moderate reform yielded to suspicion and persecution after events like the Affair of the Placards. While he maintained a largely Catholic realm, the seeds of Protestant dissent were taking root, soon to grow into a major crisis for his successors.

CHAPTER 12: THE WARS OF RELIGION AND THE REIGN OF HENRY IV

Introduction

The cultural and intellectual achievements of the French Renaissance under Francis I and Henry II did not prevent the kingdom from sliding into religious conflict. By the mid-16th century, **Protestantism**—especially Calvinism—had taken root among segments of the nobility, urban elites, and even rural populations. The Crown remained staunchly Catholic, but internal divisions at court, combined with increasing Huguenot organization, sparked a series of civil wars collectively known as the **French Wars of Religion** (1562–1598).

These conflicts pitted **Catholics** against **Huguenots** (French Calvinist Protestants) in a struggle complicated by power-hungry nobles, foreign interventions, and shifting alliances. The monarchy, initially led by weak Valois kings under the regency of Catherine de' Medici, struggled to impose order. Amid assassinations, massacres, and shifting political fortunes, France teetered on the brink of disintegration.

Eventually, **Henry of Navarre**, a Huguenot prince from the Bourbon line, emerged as Henry IV. His pragmatic conversion to Catholicism and the issuance of the **Edict of Nantes** (1598) ended the major phases of the wars, laying the groundwork for a revitalized monarchy. This chapter traces these turbulent decades, from the early tension under Henry II and Catherine de' Medici to the final triumph of Henry IV, examining how religious strife reshaped France's political landscape and tested the monarchy's resilience.

1. Tensions Under Henry II and the Growth of Protestantism

Henry II (1547–1559)
When Francis I died in 1547, his son Henry II continued many of his father's policies,

including maintaining pressure on Protestant dissent. Henry II was a devout Catholic and formed the **Chambre Ardente** to judge heresy cases more aggressively. Yet, persecution did not stop the spread of Calvinist ideas. Huguenot congregations formed discreetly, especially in cities like Paris, Lyon, and La Rochelle.

Noble Support for Huguenots

A significant development was the **noble adoption of Protestantism**. Some aristocrats saw Calvinism as a way to resist the growing power of the Crown. Others were influenced by the theological appeal of reform. Families like the Condés and the Colignys became notable Huguenot leaders, giving the movement political and military clout. Their ability to raise private armies would later fuel open rebellion.

Peace of Cateau-Cambrésis (1559)

Henry II concluded the Peace of Cateau-Cambrésis with Spain in 1559, ending decades of conflict over Italy. This peace left France free to address internal matters. Tragically for Henry II, he died shortly afterward from a jousting accident at a tournament celebrating the peace. His unexpected death thrust the monarchy into a succession crisis. His sons—Francis II, Charles IX, and Henry III—were all minors or inexperienced rulers, placing real power in the hands of regents and influential nobles.

---

2. Francis II, Catherine de' Medici, and the Duke of Guise

Francis II's Short Reign (1559-1560)

Henry II's eldest son, **Francis II**, was only 15 when he became king. Married to Mary, Queen of Scots, Francis II fell under the sway of his wife's uncles, the **Guises**, an ultra-Catholic noble family. The Guise faction dominated the royal council, marginalizing other nobles like the Bourbons (e.g., Anthony of Navarre, Prince of Condé) who leaned Protestant.

Conspiracy of Amboise (1560)

Opponents of the Guise family, including some Huguenots, plotted to seize the young king at Amboise, hoping to free him from Guise influence. This scheme, known as the Amboise Conspiracy, failed spectacularly. The Guises responded with brutal repression, executing conspirators. Tensions soared, forcing the Crown to realize that the Protestant question could no longer be ignored. However, Francis II died in late 1560, leaving the throne to his brother, Charles IX, who was still a child.

Catherine de' Medici as Regent
With Charles IX only 10 years old, the formidable **Catherine de' Medici**—the widow of Henry II—assumed the regency. Of Italian origin, Catherine maneuvered between Catholic and Huguenot nobles, seeking to preserve Valois authority. She tried moderate policies, issuing the **Edict of January (1562)**, which granted limited toleration for Huguenot worship outside town walls. Yet such concessions enraged Catholic hardliners, setting the stage for open violence.

---

3. Outbreak of the Wars of Religion

Massacre at Vassy (March 1562)
The immediate spark for war came when the Duke of Guise's armed retinue attacked a Huguenot congregation worshipping in a barn at Vassy, killing or wounding dozens. News of the **Massacre of Vassy** electrified both sides. Huguenots, led by Louis, Prince of Condé, and Admiral Gaspard de Coligny, took up arms to defend their right to worship. Catholics rallied under the Guise banner to suppress heresy.

First War (1562–1563)
This initial conflict saw pitched battles and sieges across regions like Normandy, the Loire Valley, and southwestern towns. Catherine de' Medici, desperate to maintain order, attempted to mediate. The Edict of Amboise (1563) ended the first phase of fighting, granting restricted freedoms to Huguenots. But distrust ran deep, and local violence continued sporadically.

Rise of Factionalism
The monarchy's weakness encouraged noble factions to seek foreign support. Huguenot leaders forged alliances with Protestant states in Germany and England, hoping for money and troops. The Catholic side sometimes looked to Spain or the papacy. These entanglements internationalized the French conflict, making the wars more protracted and devastating.

4. Escalation

Power Struggles at Court
Charles IX reached his teenage years, but real power remained with Catherine de' Medici and competing noble factions. The Guises continued to champion strict Catholicism, while the Bourbon-Condé axis led the Huguenots. Admiral Coligny emerged as a key Protestant strategist, advocating a plan to relieve French Protestants from persecution and to confront external Catholic threats (notably Spain).

Second War (1567–1568)
Rising tensions led the Huguenots to launch a surprise attempt to capture the king in what was called the **Surprise of Meaux (1567)**. Though the plan failed, it triggered renewed fighting. Battles raged in multiple provinces. Once again, Catherine sought a negotiated peace, resulting in the **Peace of Longjumeau (1568)**, which again offered limited Huguenot concessions. Neither side felt satisfied, setting the stage for more conflict.

Third War (1568–1570)
Fears of Spanish intervention and the assassin's murder of key Huguenot figures escalated matters. Fighting resumed, with Protestant forces rallying in strongholds like La Rochelle. The monarchy faced financial strains, unable to pay for sustained warfare. The **Peace of Saint-Germain-en-Laye (1570)** ended the third conflict, granting Huguenots freedom of worship in specific cities, plus the right to fortify certain towns for security. This was a high point for Huguenot political power.

---

5. St. Bartholomew's Day Massacre

Royal Marriage as a Gesture of Peace
In August 1572, Catherine de' Medici orchestrated the marriage of her daughter, **Margaret of Valois**, to the Huguenot prince **Henry of Navarre** (later Henry IV). This union aimed to reconcile Catholics and Protestants, bringing a leading Huguenot into the royal family. Many prominent Huguenots, including Admiral Coligny, arrived in Paris for the wedding celebrations.

Tensions in Paris
Despite the festive atmosphere, Paris was a staunchly Catholic city. Radical

preachers inflamed public opinion against the presence of so many Huguenot nobles. Factions within the royal court worried that Coligny, a trusted adviser to Charles IX, was steering the king toward war with Spain to aid Protestant rebels in the Netherlands. Catherine de' Medici, fearing Coligny's influence, plotted his removal.

The Massacre
Shortly after the wedding, a failed assassination attempt on Coligny heightened tensions. Then, on the night of August 23-24, 1572—**St. Bartholomew's Day**—royal guards and Catholic mobs attacked Huguenot leaders, including Coligny, who was murdered. The violence spread through the streets of Paris, killing thousands of Protestants. Massacres rippled out to other French cities over the following weeks, resulting in an unknown but significant death toll.

National Shock and International Reaction
The St. Bartholomew's Day Massacre shocked Europe. Catholics supportive of a harsh line claimed it was necessary to prevent a Huguenot coup, while Protestants saw it as a brutal, premeditated slaughter. King Charles IX, possibly complicit or manipulated, took responsibility, further tarnishing the monarchy's image. Many Huguenots fled abroad or retreated to strongholds like La Rochelle. What began as a forced attempt to eliminate leading Huguenots turned into one of the most infamous episodes of religious violence in 16th-century Europe.

---

6. The War of the Three Henrys

Gradual Shift Under Henry III
After Charles IX died in 1574, his brother became **Henry III**. Educated and intelligent, Henry III faced a kingdom fractured by religious and political rivalry. He attempted moderate policies, but extremist factions on both sides undermined stability. The ultra-Catholic **Holy League**, led initially by the Duke of Guise, demanded no compromise with Protestants. Meanwhile, Huguenots regrouped under Henry of Navarre.

Henry of Navarre
By inheritance, Henry of Navarre (a distant relative of the Valois) was next in line to the throne if Henry III died childless. A Huguenot, Henry of Navarre thus posed a direct threat to ultra-Catholics who refused a Protestant king. This succession

crisis fueled tensions, especially after the death of Francis, Duke of Alençon (the king's last brother) in 1584. With no closer Valois heirs, Henry of Navarre became heir presumptive.

Formation of the Holy League

The Duke of Guise formed the **Catholic League** (or Holy League) to block Henry of Navarre's succession. The League received covert support from Philip II of Spain, who wanted a strongly Catholic France aligned with Spanish policy. From 1585 onward, the country spiraled into a renewed civil war known as the **War of the Three Henrys**:

1. **Henry III** (the reigning king, seeking to maintain the monarchy).
2. **Henry of Guise** (leading the Catholic League).
3. **Henry of Navarre** (leading the Huguenots and rightful heir).

Assassinations and Chaos

As fighting raged, Henry III tried to balance the factions. Under pressure from the League, he expelled Huguenots from royal offices, but also resented the Guise family's usurpation of authority in Paris. In 1588, Henry III orchestrated the assassination of Henry of Guise in the royal palace. This shocking act turned many Parisians against the king, who fled the capital. Meanwhile, Henry of Navarre advanced militarily, securing alliances in southwestern regions.

Death of Henry III (1589)

The final blow came in 1589, when a fanatical Catholic friar assassinated Henry III. Dying without heirs, Henry III recognized Henry of Navarre as his successor. Thus, the Huguenot leader became **Henry IV** of France, but faced a kingdom largely controlled by the Catholic League and uncertain provincial loyalties.

---

7. Henry IV's Path to the Throne and Conversion

Military Campaigns

To claim his crown, Henry IV needed to defeat the Catholic League and secure the recognition of Catholic France. He won key battles, such as **Arques (1589)** and **Ivry (1590)**, demonstrating capable leadership. Nonetheless, capturing Paris proved difficult, as the capital remained fiercely League-aligned, supported by Spanish troops and resolute Catholic citizens.

"Paris is Worth a Mass"
Realizing that most French people were Catholic, Henry IV famously decided to **convert to Catholicism** in 1593. Whether out of genuine conviction or political pragmatism, this conversion removed the main obstacle to acceptance by moderate Catholics. As he allegedly said, "Paris is worth a Mass." Over time, leading Catholic nobles acknowledged him as king, and Spanish support for the League waned.

Coronation and Consolidation
In 1594, Henry IV entered Paris to popular acclaim from weary citizens craving peace. He was formally crowned at Chartres Cathedral (Reims was still in disrepair from the wars). Gradually, provincial strongholds recognized his authority. By the late 1590s, Henry had subdued most pockets of League resistance, either through negotiations or military action. The monarchy's unity was reestablished, though the scars of war persisted in many devastated regions.

---

8. The Edict of Nantes and Religious Settlement

A Compromise Document
To end the decades of civil strife, Henry IV issued the **Edict of Nantes** in 1598. This edict granted Huguenots the right to private worship throughout the kingdom and public worship in specified locations. They were allowed to maintain a number of fortified towns for self-defense, such as La Rochelle and Montauban. Huguenots also received civil rights, including the ability to hold public office.

Balancing Catholic Opinion
While the Edict safeguarded Huguenot religious freedoms, Catholicism remained the official religion of the kingdom. Catholic clergy retained privileges, and Catholic worship was mandatory at the royal court. The king hoped this middle path would appease moderate Catholics who wanted unity, while stopping short of giving Huguenots too much power.

Reaction to the Edict
Many Catholics accepted it grudgingly as the price of peace. Hardcore Catholics protested that the Crown was tolerating heresy. Meanwhile, some Protestants wanted even broader rights. Despite criticisms from both extremes, the Edict of Nantes was a milestone in religious toleration, offering a fragile coexistence that would hold for much of the 17th century.

9. Henry IV's Reforms and the Restoration of Royal Authority

Economic and Social Rebuilding

Once the wars ended, Henry IV focused on rebuilding the shattered kingdom. He appointed **Maximilien de Béthune, Duke of Sully**, as his chief minister. Sully streamlined taxes and curbed wasteful spending. Encouraging agriculture, commerce, and infrastructure, the government repaired roads and bridges, supported irrigation projects, and promoted the planting of mulberry trees for silkworm cultivation.

Promotion of Trade and Industry

To revive urban centers, Henry IV boosted trade, supporting merchants and guilds. Sully advanced mercantilist ideas, believing in a favorable balance of trade. France resumed exporting wine, salt, and luxury goods. The monarchy also pursued colonial ventures, though on a smaller scale than Spain or Portugal, laying early claims in Canada.

Noble Relations

Henry IV sought to reconcile with former League nobles. By offering pardons, titles, and financial rewards, he brought them back into the royal fold. Some Huguenot leaders likewise received offices and honors. This inclusive approach gradually healed the monarchy's relationship with both Catholic and Protestant aristocrats, though resentment lingered in some corners.

Paris as a Royal Capital

Henry IV famously declared, "I want there to be no peasant in my kingdom so poor that he cannot have a chicken in his pot on Sundays." Though partially symbolic, this sentiment reflected his desire to be seen as a caring monarch. He improved Paris's infrastructure, commissioning the construction of the **Pont Neuf** bridge, paving streets, and encouraging new residential quarters. The city, relieved from years of League domination, began to flourish again.

10. The Legacy of the Wars of Religion

Human and Material Costs
From 1562 to 1598, an estimated three million people died directly or indirectly due to the Wars of Religion—through battle casualties, massacres, famine, and disease. Many towns and rural districts were ruined. The kingdom's finances were deeply strained, forcing repeated debasements of the currency and emergency taxes. Social trust eroded, as neighbor fought neighbor over confessional allegiance.

Shift in Political Thought
The wars prompted debates on the nature of monarchy and resistance. Huguenot writers like **François Hotman** (*Franco-Gallia*) and **Theodore Beza** justified rebellion under certain conditions, arguing that kings had to respect subjects' rights to religious freedom. Conversely, Catholic theorists supported absolute monarchy or championed the League's right to depose a heretical or weak ruler. Over time, a new concept of **royal absolutism** emerged, wherein the Crown claimed ultimate authority to guarantee peace, bridging the religious divide.

Rise of the Bourbon Dynasty
With Henry IV, the Bourbon branch came to the throne, ushering a line of kings that would guide France through the 17th and 18th centuries. By ending the civil wars and issuing the Edict of Nantes, Henry IV restored monarchy's prestige. Although he was tragically assassinated in 1610 by a Catholic fanatic, Henry IV left a kingdom far more stable than he had found it.

Road to Future Absolutism
The monarchy's survival through these brutal conflicts demonstrated that only strong royal power could hold France together. This lesson carried over to the next generation, influencing Louis XIII and especially Louis XIV, who would later perfect the system of absolute monarchy. The monarchy's determination to control religious strife also set a precedent for centralized intervention in faith matters, leading to later revocations of the Edict of Nantes—but, for now, Henry IV's solution allowed France a period of relative tranquility.

CHAPTER 13: THE BOURBON DYNASTY AND THE REIGN OF LOUIS XIII

Introduction

The assassination of King Henry IV in 1610 ended the life of a monarch who had restored stability to France following the brutal Wars of Religion. Henry's pragmatic leadership, exemplified by the Edict of Nantes (1598), had granted a fragile coexistence between Catholics and Huguenots, and his reforms spurred economic recovery. Upon his death, the Crown passed to his nine-year-old son, **Louis XIII**. This abrupt transition threatened to undo Henry's achievements if factional strife or foreign powers intervened.

Over the next three decades, France would face significant internal and external challenges. During Louis XIII's minority, the regency of his mother, **Marie de' Medici**, struggled with noble unrest. Later, Louis XIII and his chief minister, **Cardinal Richelieu**, gradually imposed stronger central authority, reduced the power of the Huguenot strongholds, and positioned France as a leading European power in the Thirty Years' War. By the king's death in 1643, the foundations for absolute monarchy were largely in place, setting the stage for the next reign—Louis XIV.

This chapter examines Louis XIII's accession, the regency under Marie de' Medici, the ascendancy of Cardinal Richelieu, the conflicts with Huguenot enclaves, and France's interventions in Europe's religious wars. Through these tumultuous decades, the Bourbon monarchy strengthened its hold, forging the path toward a more centralized France.

1. The Regency of Marie de' Medici

A Child King and a Queen Regent

When Henry IV died, the new king, Louis XIII, was too young to rule independently. His mother, **Marie de' Medici**, became regent. Marie, originally from Florence, had served mostly in a ceremonial role during Henry's reign. Now thrust into leadership, she had to maintain Henry IV's policies—especially the Edict of Nantes—while grappling with restless nobles who saw an opportunity to regain influence.

Marie's position was insecure. The late king had been beloved by many for ending the civil wars. Certain noble factions, notably those led by the Prince of Condé and other high-born aristocrats, doubted Marie's ability to govern. They tried to pressure or manipulate the regent, demanding pensions, offices, and political concessions.

Conciliation with Spain

One of Marie de' Medici's key moves was a rapprochement with the **Spanish Habsburgs**, a family Henry IV had often viewed warily. Marie arranged a double marriage treaty:

1. Louis XIII was betrothed to the Spanish Infanta, Anne of Austria.
2. The king's sister, Elizabeth of France, was promised to the future Philip IV of Spain.

These matches aimed to secure peace along France's southern border and reduce Spanish interference in French affairs. However, many patriotic nobles and ministers considered it a betrayal of Henry IV's more independent stance. Distrust of Spanish influence would linger throughout Louis XIII's early years, coloring the monarchy's relationships with both domestic and foreign powers.

Noble Revolts and Court Intrigue

Despite her efforts, Marie's regency faced multiple **noble revolts**. High lords demanded a voice in policy or used the regency's weakness to expand their provincial authority. Some withheld tax revenues or mustered private militias. Marie tried to buy them off with titles and royal favor. This approach sapped the treasury and granted unscrupulous nobles undue leverage.

Internal court rivalries also plagued the regency. Marie relied on favorites like **Concino Concini**, an Italian-born courtier who rose to the rank of Marshal d'Ancre. Concini's power and foreign roots irritated many French nobles. Condé, for instance, launched an uprising (1614–1615) which forced the regent to summon the **Estates-General**—the last time this assembly would convene before 1789. The Estates-General met in 1614 but made no lasting reforms, as competing factions paralyzed effective action.

Louis XIII's Coming of Age

In 1615, Louis XIII turned 14, the traditional age of majority for a French king. Yet Marie and her circle still kept him sidelined. Growing resentful, the adolescent Louis formed his own clique, chafing at Concini's dominance. In 1617, with support from trusted courtiers, Louis XIII engineered Concini's arrest and assassination. He then banished his mother to Blois, seizing personal control of government. This dramatic coup ended Marie's regency and marked the real beginning of Louis XIII's reign.

---

2. Early Reign of Louis XIII

Exile of Marie de' Medici

Having ousted Concini, Louis XIII sidelined his mother's allies. Marie's captivity in Blois alienated her supporters, including some princes of the blood and Italian confidants. Over time, the king recognized the need for a more stable reconciliation. In 1619, he permitted his mother to relocate, eventually granting partial restoration of her privileges. Still, their relationship remained tense, with repeated cycles of conflict and reconciliation.

Favorites and Ministers

Louis XIII, like many monarchs, relied on influential "favorites." Initially, the young king favored **Charles d'Albert, Duke of Luynes**, who helped orchestrate Concini's downfall. Luynes became a key advisor and soared to high office. However, he lacked the skill to manage deeper problems, such as Huguenot unrest and noble rivalries.

When Luynes died in 1621, Louis XIII began looking for alternative ministers. Various nobles vied for influence, but none displayed the administrative brilliance or political cunning needed to stabilize the realm. This environment paved the way for the eventual rise of **Armand Jean du Plessis, Cardinal Richelieu**—initially a protégé of Marie de' Medici—who would become the architect of royal centralization.

Huguenot Tensions Increase

While Henry IV's Edict of Nantes had given Huguenots a measure of toleration and fortified towns, deep suspicions remained. Many Catholics disliked these enclaves, fearing a "state within a state." For their part, Huguenots resented the monarchy's drift away from Henry IV's protective stance, especially as local governors harassed Protestant worship or restricted their fortifications.

From 1621 to 1622, a short conflict erupted when Huguenot leaders resisted the king's attempts to diminish their autonomy. La Rochelle, a major Protestant port, refused to submit fully to the Crown. Royal troops subdued some strongholds, but the monarchy, lacking a powerful central minister or consistent strategy, settled on compromises that left underlying tensions unresolved.

---

3. The Rise of Cardinal Richelieu

Background and Early Service

Armand Jean du Plessis, Cardinal Richelieu, first gained notice serving in the Estates-General of 1614, where he demonstrated keen political skill. Initially a bishop, he became a favorite of Marie de' Medici, who helped him secure a cardinal's hat. Although he lost influence during the struggle between Louis XIII and Marie, Richelieu maneuvered back into the royal council around 1624, thanks to his diplomatic abilities.

As Louis XIII's chief minister, Richelieu had two overarching goals:

1. **Strengthen royal authority internally** by reducing the power of nobles and the political rights of Huguenots.
2. **Enhance France's position in Europe** by countering Habsburg supremacy, especially as the Thirty Years' War engulfed the Holy Roman Empire.

Suppression of the Huguenot Strongholds

Richelieu saw the Huguenot enclaves as a direct challenge to royal sovereignty. Although France still officially upheld the Edict of Nantes' religious protections, Richelieu insisted that Protestants not possess separate political or military privileges. The most crucial confrontation occurred at **La Rochelle**, a wealthy maritime city that had become the de facto center of Huguenot political power.

- **Siege of La Rochelle (1627–1628)**: When La Rochelle aligned with England (which sent ships to aid the Protestant defenders), Richelieu directed a massive siege. He built fortifications, blockaded the port, and starved the city. After 14 months of resistance, La Rochelle surrendered in October 1628. The monarchy dismantled its walls and took direct control, ending the city's semi-autonomous status.
- **Peace of Alais (1629)**: In the aftermath, Richelieu granted **Peace of Alais**, which confirmed Huguenots' right to worship but stripped them of fortified cities and political assemblies. This effectively ended the era of Huguenot "state within a state." While Protestants could still practice their faith (as outlined in the Edict of Nantes), they lost military autonomy.

Reining in Noble Power

Simultaneously, Richelieu confronted rebellious nobles who had grown accustomed to extorting favors from weak regencies. He employed **intendants**—royal officials sent to provinces with broad administrative powers—to curtail the old feudal lords' authority. These intendants reported directly to Richelieu, collecting taxes, overseeing justice, and policing local elites.

Prominent nobles who challenged the Crown found themselves imprisoned or executed. Richelieu famously stated the monarchy's aim to "break down the great and raise up the small," meaning to dismantle overmighty subjects and empower loyal servants of the king. This policy sparked conspiracies against Richelieu's life, but Louis XIII backed his chief minister, valuing results over the nobles' grievances.

4. France in the Thirty Years' War

Overview of the Conflict

The **Thirty Years' War** (1618–1648) began in the Holy Roman Empire as a primarily religious dispute between Catholic and Protestant states. Soon, dynastic and geopolitical rivalries turned it into a broader European war. The Habsburgs, ruling Spain and Austria, sought to maintain dominance in central Europe and the Spanish Netherlands.

Richelieu, though Catholic, supported the policy of weakening Habsburg power, which threatened to encircle France. Initially, France financed Protestant allies (like Sweden under Gustavus Adolphus) to fight the Austrian Habsburgs. But in 1635, France formally joined the war, opening direct hostilities against Spain in the Low Countries and along the Pyrenees.

Military Campaigns and Challenges

French armies had mixed success. They captured some fortresses in the Spanish Netherlands, but faced strong resistance from experienced Spanish tercios. In the Rhineland and northern Italy, France fought Austrian Habsburg forces. The war drained the royal treasury, requiring new taxes and forced loans from nobles. Despite these strains, Richelieu believed that victory or at least a favorable peace was crucial for France's long-term security.

Internal Unrest

The prolonged conflict led to heavy taxation, which sparked revolts in various regions. Peasants who could barely afford the taille or gabelle rose up in local insurrections. Richelieu's intendants suppressed these uprisings harshly. Meanwhile, some noble conspiracies reemerged, fueled by dissatisfaction over the war's burden. Nevertheless, Richelieu's spy networks and the unwavering support of Louis XIII ensured that these rebellions did not topple the regime.

5. The Growth of Centralized Authority and Court Culture

Royal Authority Strengthened

By the late 1630s, the monarchy had made significant strides in centralizing authority:

1. **Intendant System**: Extended widely, overshadowing regional governors.
2. **Legal and Judicial Reforms**: Royal courts enforced the king's edicts, limiting the autonomy of local parlements which occasionally resisted.
3. **Religious Uniformity**: The Peace of Alais had curtailed Huguenot political power, while Catholic institutions largely supported the Crown, especially under Richelieu's guidance.

Yet, the monarchy still had to tread carefully. Overly oppressive tax demands could provoke deeper revolts, and any sign of weakness might incite powerful nobles or Spanish armies to strike.

Patronage of the Arts

Despite the war, Louis XIII and Richelieu promoted cultural achievements. Richelieu himself was a patron of letters, founding the **Académie Française** in 1635 to standardize the French language and encourage literary excellence. Influential playwrights like **Pierre Corneille** arose during this period, reflecting the monarchy's desire to showcase a refined national culture.

Louis XIII, though overshadowed by the flamboyant reign of his father and the future Louis XIV, also commissioned artworks and music to enhance the Crown's prestige. Baroque influences reached France, blending religious grandeur with royal propaganda. Many of these projects foreshadowed the artistic explosion under Louis XIV.

Queen Anne of Austria and the Royal Family

Louis XIII's marriage to **Anne of Austria**, arranged in his youth under the Spanish alliance, produced no children for many years, fueling succession worries. Their relationship was often strained, as the queen felt isolated and overshadowed by Richelieu's dominance. Nevertheless, in 1638, after over 20 years of marriage, Anne gave birth to a son—**Louis Dieudonné**, the future Louis XIV. Two years later, another son, Philippe, was born. This miraculous late arrival of heirs stabilized the Bourbon line and gave Richelieu new impetus to secure the monarchy's future.

6. The Final Years of Richelieu and Louis XIII

Richelieu's Declining Health

Cardinal Richelieu, never robust in health, struggled with severe ailments by the early 1640s. Yet he refused to relinquish power, continuing to direct France's war efforts and internal reforms. He promoted **Jules Mazarin**, an Italian-born diplomat, to assist him at court, ensuring continuity of policies once he passed.

In 1642, another conspiracy emerged, this time involving the king's brother Gaston d'Orléans and the king's favorite, the Marquis de Cinq-Mars. Richelieu exposed the plot. Cinq-Mars was executed, and Gaston forced into submission. This final triumph affirmed Richelieu's iron grip, but the cardinal died in December of the same year, leaving Mazarin as his successor in counsel to the king.

Death of Louis XIII (1643)

Louis XIII, afflicted by chronic tuberculosis, died in April 1643, only a few months after Richelieu. Although overshadowed by the cardinal's forceful personality, Louis XIII had played a crucial role in supporting Richelieu's reforms and repressions, ensuring that the monarchy emerged more centralized than at any time since the Middle Ages.

At the time of his death, Louis XIII left the throne to his four-year-old son, Louis Dieudonné—who would ascend as **Louis XIV**. The regency fell to Queen Anne of Austria. She, along with Cardinal Mazarin, would guide the kingdom through the concluding phases of the Thirty Years' War and into the next era of monarchical power.

7. Significance of the Reign of Louis XIII

Centralization and the Path to Absolutism
Under Henry IV, the monarchy had recovered from civil wars, but it still faced

strong feudal structures. During Louis XIII's reign, Richelieu's systematic policies dismantled many autonomous enclaves—both Huguenot and noble. The Crown's army grew more permanent, financed by direct taxes. The network of intendants offered a new mechanism of local governance, bypassing the old nobility. While the monarchy did not yet reach the full might of "absolutism," the blueprint was in place for the more forceful rule of Louis XIV.

Religious Unification
The Peace of Alais maintained the Edict of Nantes in principle, but effectively ended Protestant political autonomy. This shaped a single national authority in matters of state, though private conscience was, for the time being, respected. The monarchy signaled that religious pluralism would be tolerated only insofar as it did not undermine royal sovereignty.

Foreign Engagement
France's entry into the Thirty Years' War revealed the monarchy's ambition to break Habsburg encirclement. Though expensive and complex, this involvement eventually improved France's diplomatic standing. By the time of the Peace of Westphalia (1648), France had achieved many of Richelieu's strategic goals, setting itself up as a prime influencer in European affairs.

Cultural Foundations
Despite warfare and political turmoil, France witnessed the rise of new literary and artistic currents. Richelieu's creation of the Académie Française promoted linguistic unity and literary culture under royal oversight. Composers, painters, architects, and writers found patronage at court, beginning a trend that would reach its zenith under Louis XIV's lavish sponsorship.

CHAPTER 14: THE AGE OF LOUIS XIV AND ABSOLUTISM

Introduction

Few reigns in European history rival the length or impact of **Louis XIV** (1643–1715). Referred to as the "Sun King," Louis XIV oversaw the height of Bourbon absolutism in France. Building upon the centralizing reforms of Cardinal Richelieu and Louis XIII, he consolidated royal power to an unprecedented level, subordinating nobles, revoking Huguenot rights, and waging wars that shaped Europe's balance of power.

This chapter examines the trajectory of Louis XIV's reign, from his minority under the regency of his mother, **Anne of Austria**, and Cardinal Mazarin, to his personal assumption of power, the construction of **Versailles**, and his aggressive foreign policy. We will see how these actions influenced French society, culture, and government. Though the Sun King's wars and extravagant spending strained the kingdom, his reign transformed France into the preeminent power of continental Europe and left a lasting cultural legacy.

1. The Regency of Anne of Austria and Cardinal Mazarin

A Child King Ascends

When Louis XIII died in 1643, his son, **Louis XIV**, was only four years old. The queen mother, **Anne of Austria**, assumed the regency. She set aside her late husband's will, which had attempted to limit her power by creating a regency council. Instead, Anne took full control and placed her trust in **Cardinal Jules Mazarin**, Richelieu's protégé.

Mazarin, originally from Italy, faced considerable hostility from French nobles who resented a foreign-born minister. Nonetheless, he shared Richelieu's vision of a strong monarchy. He continued France's involvement in the **Thirty Years' War**, striving to secure favorable peace terms that would enhance French power.

The End of the Thirty Years' War

Mazarin and Anne steered France through the final years of Europe's cataclysmic conflict. By the **Peace of Westphalia (1648)**, France gained territories in the Rhineland (like Alsace) and significantly curtailed Habsburg influence in Germany. This diplomatic triumph signaled France's emergence as a principal European power. However, war with Spain continued beyond 1648, only concluding with the **Peace of the Pyrenees (1659)**, which brought further gains, including territory in the Spanish Netherlands and marriage arrangements beneficial to France.

Financial Burdens and Taxation

These military successes came at a steep cost. The Crown financed war efforts through heavy taxes. Peasant revolts erupted in various provinces, protesting the taille and indirect levies. The monarchy raised revenue also by selling offices, an approach that undercut administrative efficiency and prompted corruption. As the monarchy demanded more funds, tensions rose between Mazarin and high courts like the **Parlement of Paris**, which sought to limit royal edicts on new taxes or legal reforms.

---

2. The Fronde

Causes of the Fronde

The **Fronde**—a series of civil disturbances from 1648 to 1653—stemmed from resistance to royal centralization and financial exactions. It took two forms:

1. **Fronde Parlementaire (1648–1649)**: The Parlement of Paris and other courts refused to register new taxes, asserting traditional rights. They demanded reduced financial burdens and a check on the Crown's authority.
2. **Fronde des Nobles (1650–1653)**: Disgruntled princes and magnates, such as the Prince of Condé, led armed revolts to regain feudal privileges or seize power from Mazarin's government.

Early Victories and Subsequent Chaos

In 1648, the Parlement of Paris forced Mazarin and Anne to make concessions, prompting popular uprisings in Paris. The royal family fled the capital, reminiscent of the earlier upheavals under Louis XIII. Encouraged by the success of the courts, nobles launched their own revolts. However, internal divisions plagued the rebels—parlementarians disagreed with ambitious princes who aimed to dominate the Crown rather than simply reform it.

The young Louis XIV endured the humiliations of flight and near-capture. These experiences would later shape his determination to break noble power and move his court away from potentially rebellious Paris.

Restoration of Royal Authority

By 1653, the Crown regained the upper hand. Mazarin maneuvered diplomatically, making separate treaties with some rebel nobles, offering bribes or pardons. Royal forces recaptured strongholds. The lack of a united front among the Frondeurs doomed their cause. Commoners, fed up with prolonged disorder, also turned against the rebels.

Mazarin reentered Paris triumphantly, reaffirming the monarchy's primacy. The Fronde's failure reinforced the lesson that strong central government was essential for stability. Many nobles realized they could not overthrow the Crown, leading them instead to seek favor at court. This shift paved the way for Louis XIV's later style of governance, in which great lords vied for prestige at Versailles rather than waging open war.

---

3. Louis XIV's Personal Rule

Mazarin's Death and the King's Announcement

Cardinal Mazarin died in March 1661. Soon after, the 22-year-old **Louis XIV** astonished his ministers by announcing he would rule without a chief minister. Claiming his authority as derived directly from God, he declared, "I am the State" (or in French lore, "L'État, c'est moi"—though he might not have said those exact words). From that moment, Louis XIV made all significant decisions, assisted by councils of loyal secretaries rather than a single all-powerful minister.

This break from the tradition of Richelieu and Mazarin signaled the king's intent to establish an unambiguous, **absolute monarchy**, free from overshadowing advisors. In practice, Louis XIV delegated day-to-day tasks to skilled men like **Jean-Baptiste**

Colbert (finance), **François-Michel le Tellier de Louvois** (war), and **Hugues de Lionne** (foreign affairs), but they remained firmly under the king's supervision.

Centralizing Reforms

Louis XIV took immediate steps to tighten royal control:

- **Tax and Financial Reform**: Jean-Baptiste Colbert tackled corruption in tax farming, sought to expand the Crown's direct tax base, and introduced mercantilist policies promoting domestic manufacturing.
- **Army Organization**: Louvois professionalized the military with better training, supply systems, and promotions based on merit (though noble birth remained important). This produced a formidable army loyal to the Crown.
- **Regional Governance**: Intendants continued to monitor provinces, overshadowing traditional noble governors. The Crown repressed local parlements whenever they blocked royal edicts.

These measures built upon Richelieu's legacy but reached new heights as the king demanded absolute obedience from every level of governance.

---

4. The Court at Versailles

Building the Palace

One of Louis XIV's most enduring legacies is the **Palace of Versailles**, located about 20 kilometers southwest of Paris. Initially a modest hunting lodge built by Louis XIII, Versailles underwent massive expansions beginning in the 1660s. The king sought a lavish setting that showcased his glory and kept the high nobility within his watchful gaze.

The architecture at Versailles combined **Baroque** grandeur with classical symmetry, featuring vast wings, ornate gardens designed by **André Le Nôtre**, and the famous Hall of Mirrors (Galerie des Glaces). Thousands of workers toiled for decades, draining marshland, constructing fountains, and rearranging entire landscapes to reflect Louis XIV's desire for perfect order—symbolic of his control over France.

The Role of the Nobility at Court

Versailles functioned as more than a royal residence. It served as a **political theater**. Louis XIV invited (and often compelled) leading nobles to reside there, entangling them in an elaborate system of court etiquette. Dukes and princes sought the privilege of handing the king his shirt or lighting his candle—seemingly trivial tasks that conferred prestige.

This **court culture** distracted nobles from plotting rebellions by immersing them in social rituals, gossip, and endless ceremonies. The king awarded pensions, offices, and honors to those who pleased him, transforming the nobility into courtiers dependent on royal favor. This arrangement reduced their capacity to lead provincial revolts, aligning them closer to the Crown's centralized power.

Artistic Patronage and the "Sun King" Image

Versailles also became a stage for lavish **ballets, operas, and plays**. Louis XIV himself performed in ballets during his youth, earning the nickname "Sun King" from a role portraying the rising sun. He patronized the arts extensively:

- **Jean-Baptiste Lully**: Composed court music and operas, establishing a French baroque style.
- **Molière**: Wrote comedic plays such as *Tartuffe*, *Le Misanthrope*, and *Le Bourgeois gentilhomme*, performed at court.
- **Racine** and **Corneille**: Produced classical tragedies that exalted the state's ideals of order and grandeur.

Through these cultural pursuits, Louis XIV broadcast the monarchy's supremacy and refined taste, shaping French culture for generations.

---

5. Religious Policy

Tension with Huguenots

Although Louis XIII and Richelieu had reduced Huguenot political power, the Edict of Nantes still guaranteed limited religious freedoms. Louis XIV, however, pursued religious uniformity, believing that a single faith underpinned a stable monarchy. He introduced policies that harassed Huguenot communities: quartering soldiers in

Protestant homes, denying them certain professions, and offering financial incentives for conversion.

Final Revocation (1685)

In 1685, Louis XIV issued the **Edict of Fontainebleau**, also known as the **Revocation of the Edict of Nantes**. It banned Protestant worship, ordered the destruction of Huguenot churches, and closed Protestant schools. Pastors had to convert or leave the kingdom. Many Huguenots—estimates range from 200,000 to 300,000—fled France, settling in Protestant lands like the Netherlands, Brandenburg-Prussia, England, and America.

This revocation cost France a productive segment of the population, including skilled artisans and merchants. Although Louis XIV believed it showcased his piety, the policy damaged France's economic vitality and international reputation. Foreign Protestant powers grew more hostile, while within France, clandestine Protestant worship continued, albeit in fear.

---

6. Foreign Wars and Expansion

The War of Devolution (1667–1668)

Louis XIV's first major war, the **War of Devolution**, sprang from a claim that his wife, Maria Theresa of Spain, should inherit the Spanish Netherlands upon her father's death. French armies quickly overran towns in Flanders and the Franche-Comté. However, a coalition of European powers, including England and the Dutch Republic, forced Louis XIV to accept a compromise peace, ceding some conquests but retaining others.

The Dutch War (1672–1678)

Eager to punish the Dutch Republic for opposing him, Louis XIV invaded the Netherlands in 1672. Initially successful, the French faced severe resistance when the Dutch flooded their own lands to stop the advance. The war dragged on, drawing in Spain and the Holy Roman Empire. By the **Treaty of Nijmegen (1678–1679)**, France gained Franche-Comté and several border fortresses, solidifying its northeast frontier. This success enhanced Louis XIV's prestige but raised suspicion among neighboring states.

The War of the League of Augsburg (1688–1697)

Rising alarm at French aggression led to the formation of the **League of Augsburg**—an anti-French coalition including the Holy Roman Empire, Spain, the Dutch Republic, and later England under William III. The war erupted in 1688 and saw widespread fighting in the Rhineland and the Low Countries. After years of costly campaigns, the conflict ended with the **Treaty of Ryswick (1697)**, which largely restored pre-war borders. Although France retained some strategic fortresses, the war signaled that Europe had united to contain Louis XIV's expansions.

The War of the Spanish Succession (1701–1714)

The gravest conflict of Louis XIV's reign began when the childless **Charles II of Spain** named Louis XIV's grandson, Philip of Anjou, as his heir. If Philip inherited the vast Spanish empire, Europe feared a Franco-Spanish superstate. England, the Dutch Republic, Austria, and others formed the **Grand Alliance** to prevent this union.

- **Early Stages**: French armies initially performed well but soon faced defeats by the Duke of Marlborough (England) and Prince Eugene of Savoy (Austria). Key battles like Blenheim (1704), Ramillies (1706), and Malplaquet (1709) dealt severe blows to French forces.
- **Domestic Hardships**: France suffered famines, financial collapse, and war exhaustion. The government devalued currency and borrowed heavily. Morale plummeted, and even Versailles struggled to maintain its lavish routines.
- **Treaties of Utrecht (1713) and Rastatt (1714)**: Eventually, war-weary powers negotiated. Philip of Anjou became **Philip V of Spain** but renounced any future claim to the French throne, thus preventing a dynastic union. France ceded territories in North America and Europe but preserved the Bourbon seat on the Spanish throne.

Though France survived the conflict, it emerged bankrupt and drained, marking the beginning of the end for Louis XIV's unbounded ambitions.

7. The Late Reign of Louis XIV

Economic Pressures

Continuous warfare and extravagant court expenditures crippled French finances. Colbert's mercantilist policies had initially boosted manufacturing and trade, but later wars nullified many gains. High taxes and enforced loans bred resentment among peasants and townspeople. Agriculture stagnated due to soldier requisitions and neglected infrastructure. In the final decades of Louis XIV's reign, revenue shortfalls forced repeated financial improvisations.

Social Discontent

Nobles at Versailles enjoyed privileges and pensions, but lesser aristocrats and commoners felt the burdens of taxation and conscription. Rural riots occasionally flared up. Although the monarchy suppressed revolts effectively, signs of deeper social and economic strains were evident. The monarchy's image also suffered from religious persecution, with Catholics uneasy about the revocation's cruelty while Protestants faced exile or secret worship.

Court Culture and Intellectual Achievements

Despite hardships, the final years of Louis XIV's reign continued to foster remarkable cultural production. The Académie Française upheld linguistic standards, while composers like **François Couperin** flourished. Writers such as **La Fontaine** composed fables that subtly critiqued society. The "Great Century" (Grand Siècle) encompassed architects, painters, and dramatists who shaped French classicism's polished style.

French became the language of diplomacy across Europe, and Versailles served as a model for other absolutist courts, influencing palace design from Bavaria to Russia. Even enemies of France admired its sophisticated art, dance, and polite manners, testifying to Louis XIV's successful cultural diplomacy.

Personal Losses and the Succession

Louis XIV outlived most of his children and grandchildren, with multiple heirs dying from smallpox or other illnesses. In 1711 and 1712, a series of deaths took his son, the Grand Dauphin, and two grandsons, leaving only his five-year-old great-grandson, **Louis, Duke of Anjou**, to inherit the throne.

Tired and ill, Louis XIV recognized that he was leaving France burdened by debts and war fatigue. He tried to ensure a stable regency for the young heir. On his deathbed in September 1715, after a reign of 72 years, the king reputedly advised moderation in warfare and generosity toward the people—ironic counsel given his own bellicose and grandiose legacy.

Conclusion

The era of **Louis XIV** stands as a defining epoch in the history of France—one where the monarchy reached a peak of **absolutist rule**, overshadowing the power of nobles, imposing religious uniformity, and showcasing immense cultural brilliance at Versailles. Under the Sun King's watch, France became the leading military force in Europe, though at the cost of incessant wars that left the kingdom exhausted and indebted.

Culturally, Louis XIV's patronage shaped French literature, art, music, and architecture, forging an enduring style that would influence courts across the continent. Politically, his centralizing measures and glorification of royal majesty set a template for later monarchs who sought absolute control. Socially and economically, the people bore the weight of taxes and conscription, sowing seeds of discontent that would surface in future generations.

Louis XIV's death in 1715 ended the longest reign in European history up to that point. He left France strong in prestige yet weakened economically. The Bourbon monarchy persisted but faced challenges in the 18th century under Louis XV and Louis XVI, eventually leading to the monumental transformations of the French Revolution at the century's end. Still, the "Age of Louis XIV" remains a critical chapter in French history—one that epitomizes both the achievements and the contradictions of absolute monarchy.

In the next chapter, **Chapter 15**, we will explore the **Enlightenment and the Late Bourbon Era**, examining how the intellectual currents of the 18th century intersected with an aging regime. We will see how kings like Louis XV and Louis XVI struggled to maintain authority in the face of changing ideas about government and society, setting the stage for the revolutionary upheaval that would redefine France.

CHAPTER 15: THE ENLIGHTENMENT AND THE LATE BOURBON ERA

Introduction

When Louis XIV died in 1715 after a reign of more than 70 years, France stood at a crossroads. The "Sun King" had raised France to the height of royal power and cultural brilliance, but the kingdom was also burdened by wars, debts, and an uneasy society. His successor, the five-year-old Louis XV, would inherit both the glory and the troubles of the Bourbon state.

Over the next several decades (1715–1789), France witnessed major shifts in thinking, economics, and politics. This period, often called the **Late Bourbon Era**, coincided with the **Enlightenment**, a broad intellectual movement that challenged traditional authority and championed reason, progress, and individual rights. Philosophers like Voltaire, Montesquieu, and Rousseau critiqued absolute rule and proposed new ideas about government, society, and religion. Meanwhile, financial strains, social inequalities, and administrative weaknesses accumulated, sowing the seeds for a crisis that would erupt in the French Revolution of 1789.

This chapter explores the regency after Louis XIV's death, the reigns of Louis XV and Louis XVI up to 1789, and the changing cultural and intellectual landscape known as the Enlightenment. We will see how a growing public sphere, new debates, colonial expansions, and repeated failures at reform set the stage for the dramatic transformations that lay ahead.

1. The Regency of Philippe d'Orléans

Transition to a Child King
Louis XIV's successor, **Louis XV**, was only five years old at the time of his great-grandfather's death. A regency was needed, and the late king had tried to outline a council-based arrangement limiting the power of the Duke of Orléans. However, the Parlement of Paris overturned Louis XIV's will, granting full regential

authority to **Philippe d'Orléans** (a nephew of Louis XIV). Thus began the **Regency (1715–1723)**, a period characterized by attempts to reverse some of Louis XIV's centralizing measures and manage a kingdom wearied by war and debt.

Financial Crisis and John Law's System
France emerged from Louis XIV's final years deeply in debt. Seeking a solution, the regent turned to **John Law**, a Scottish financier who believed a paper-money system could stimulate the economy. Law established the **Banque Générale** (later the Banque Royale) and launched the **Mississippi Company**, aiming to develop France's colonial holdings in North America and link the issuance of bank notes to the promise of colonial profits.

For a while, speculation soared, and many French investors rushed to buy shares, creating a financial bubble. However, by 1720, confidence collapsed, leading to the so-called **Mississippi Bubble** burst. Thousands of investors faced ruin, and public anger at Law's system undermined faith in the monarchy's economic judgment. The fiasco left the state with a tarnished reputation and few lasting reforms, forcing a return to more traditional methods of finance—heavy taxation, borrowing, and venal offices.

Polysynody and Partial Decentralization
Philippe d'Orléans also experimented with **polysynody**, an arrangement where royal authority was exercised by multiple councils composed of nobles, effectively rolling back the single-minister model championed by Richelieu and Mazarin. In theory, it allowed greater noble input and avoided the concentration of power. In practice, it slowed decision-making, fueled factional rivalry, and generated confusion in policy. By 1723, the regent abandoned polysynody, reverting to a more centralized approach.

End of the Regency
Louis XV reached his official majority at age 13 (in 1723), but remained overshadowed by older relatives and advisors. When Philippe d'Orléans died suddenly that same year, the Regency ended. While the regent's era had offered a brief glimpse of experimentation—both economic (Law's system) and political (councils)—little lasting structural change resulted. The monarchy continued to rely on the existing tax system and a complex patchwork of local privileges. Meanwhile, the general public grew wary of financial schemes and resented the ongoing burden of war debts.

2. The Early Reign of Louis XV

Cardinal Fleury as First Minister
After the regent's death, the adolescent Louis XV depended on key advisors. Among them, **André-Hercule de Fleury**, a mild-mannered bishop, rose to become the king's mentor and eventually **First Minister** in 1726. Fleury was cautious, seeking to restore the state's finances and keep France at peace. His approach aligned with a widespread desire to avoid the costly wars of the previous century. He limited expenditures, reformed parts of the tax administration, and cultivated trade, bringing a degree of stability during the 1720s and 1730s.

Peaceful Interlude and Commercial Growth
Under Fleury's guidance, France mostly stayed out of major conflicts, focusing on economic revival. The monarchy's finances improved enough to reduce certain taxes and pay down some of the debt. France's commercial and maritime presence grew, notably in the Caribbean (Saint-Domingue) and India, where French trading companies competed with British and Dutch rivals. Ports like Bordeaux and Nantes prospered from the Atlantic slave trade, while Marseille handled Mediterranean and Levantine commerce.

War of the Polish Succession (1733–1738)
Despite Fleury's peaceful intentions, dynastic concerns drew France into the **War of the Polish Succession**. When the Polish throne became vacant, France backed Stanisław Leszczyński (Louis XV's father-in-law) against Austria's preferred candidate. Military engagements occurred mostly in Italy and along the Rhine, with France clashing against Austrian Habsburg power. The final peace settlement awarded Leszczyński the nominal title of King of Poland but gave him the Duchy of Lorraine in practice—a region that, upon his death, would pass to the French crown. This outcome expanded French territory without overly draining resources, thus suiting Fleury's cautious strategy.

End of Fleury's Ministry
Cardinal Fleury died in 1743, leaving Louis XV at the age of 33. Fleury's tenure provided a relatively calm respite, bringing moderate prosperity and avoiding large-scale conflict except for Polish Succession entanglements. Yet, France's structural problems remained: the regressive tax system continued to burden peasants, privileged classes maintained exemptions, and the monarchy lacked comprehensive reforms. With Fleury gone, Louis XV faced a more complicated

international scene. A new war would soon test the kingdom's finances and his leadership.

---

3. Mid-Century Conflicts

War of the Austrian Succession (1740–1748)
In 1740, the death of Emperor Charles VI of Austria triggered a succession crisis. Prussia's Frederick the Great seized Silesia from the Habsburgs, prompting Empress Maria Theresa to seek allies. France saw an opportunity to weaken Austria by supporting Prussia and Bavaria. Louis XV entered the fray, leading to the **War of the Austrian Succession** (1740–1748). Battles raged across central Europe, the Low Countries, and northern Italy.

Though French armies achieved some victories, they failed to decisively weaken Austria. By the **Treaty of Aix-la-Chapelle (1748)**, France returned most conquests. The war's net result for France was minimal territorial gain but a heavy financial toll. This renewed sense of futility in foreign wars fostered discontent at court and among the public.

Diplomatic Revolution and the Seven Years' War (1756–1763)
Shortly after the Austrian Succession conflict, European alliances shifted drastically. France, once an enemy of the Habsburgs, signed an **alliance with Austria** in 1756, known as the **Diplomatic Revolution**. Britain, which had traditionally allied with Austria, now turned to Prussia. Soon, war erupted again: the **Seven Years' War**.

- **European Theater**: France and Austria attempted to curtail Prussia's expansion. Prussia, led by Frederick the Great and backed by British subsidies, proved resilient. Despite numerical superiority, French forces suffered defeats, partly due to poor coordination and leadership.
- **Colonial Struggles**: The war also raged globally—in North America (French and Indian War), India, and the Caribbean. Britain seized key French colonial possessions, including forts in Canada and trading outposts in India. A severe blow came with the fall of **Quebec (1759)** and **Montreal (1760)**, ending France's major presence in Canada.
- **Treaty of Paris (1763)**: The final settlement forced France to cede Canada and territories east of the Mississippi River to Britain, while Louisiana west

of the Mississippi went to Spain. France retained some Caribbean islands but lost significant prestige and revenue sources.

The Seven Years' War exposed weaknesses in French naval power, colonial administration, and war finance. The monarchy's debt skyrocketed, breeding calls for reform. The public, especially the emerging middle class, criticized the incompetence of ministers and courtiers who managed the war effort.

---

4. Social and Economic Pressures in the Late Bourbon Era

Population Growth and Agricultural Limits
Throughout the 18th century, France's population continued to expand, reaching around 25–28 million people by the 1780s—making it the most populous state in Europe. This growth intensified pressure on agricultural production. Farming methods remained traditional, with limited adoption of new techniques. Crop failures and poor harvests resulted in high food prices and periodic famines. Rural poverty and peasant grievances about feudal dues set a backdrop for potential unrest.

Tax Structure and Privilege
France's tax system placed the heaviest burden on peasants and the urban lower classes, while the nobility and clergy enjoyed exemptions. Key taxes included the **taille** (a direct land tax) and the **vingtième** (a 5% income tax), from which nobles often negotiated or resisted payment. Attempts by reform-minded ministers to broaden the tax base and include privileged estates typically ran into fierce opposition from **parlements** (regional high courts) and the nobility.

Rise of a Wealthy Bourgeoisie
Despite these imbalances, commerce and industry gradually expanded. Ports like Bordeaux, Nantes, and Le Havre prospered from the Atlantic slave trade, sugar, and coffee shipments. Lyon thrived as a hub of silk production and banking. A new class of merchants, bankers, and manufacturers—collectively known as the **bourgeoisie**—amassed fortunes, sometimes buying ennobling offices. This group resented aristocratic privilege and sought greater recognition. Their frustration contributed to a broader questioning of the old social order.

Urban Unrest

Cities such as Paris, Lyon, and Marseille grew in population. Rising prices and occasional shortages of bread—often referred to as "the people's food"—led to riots and discontent. Artisans and laborers felt squeezed by stagnant wages and high costs of living. In Paris, public opinion could shape political debates, as pamphlets and newspapers circulated Enlightenment ideas, fueling criticisms of the monarchy's failings.

---

5. The Enlightenment

Philosophes and Their Works

The **Enlightenment** was a cultural and intellectual movement spanning much of the 18th century. Its advocates, called **philosophes**, promoted reason, skepticism about tradition, and belief in human progress. Key figures included:

1. **Voltaire (François-Marie Arouet)**: Famous for satire (e.g., *Candide*) and essays attacking religious intolerance. He championed civil liberties, though he favored enlightened monarchy over radical democracy.
2. **Montesquieu (Charles-Louis de Secondat)**: In *The Spirit of the Laws* (1748), he analyzed different forms of government, advocating a separation of powers to prevent tyranny—a model later influential in modern constitutions.
3. **Jean-Jacques Rousseau**: In works like *The Social Contract* (1762), he argued that sovereignty rests with the people's "general will," challenging the notion of absolute monarchy. His ideas on equality and virtue resonated with many future revolutionaries.
4. **Denis Diderot** and **Jean le Rond d'Alembert**: Editors of the **Encyclopédie**, an ambitious project compiling human knowledge. It aimed to disseminate reason and challenge religious dogma.

Spread of Enlightenment Ideas

Enlightenment thought spread through **salons**, gatherings hosted by aristocratic or bourgeois women like Madame Geoffrin or Madame de Pompadour (a mistress of Louis XV). Philosophes mingled with nobles, officials, and foreign visitors, debating questions of politics, religion, and economics. Print culture—books, pamphlets, newspapers—flourished, despite censorship. Many works circulated clandestinely, evading royal or Church bans.

Impact on Religion and the Church

Philosophes criticized religious intolerance, the union of Church and state, and clerical privilege. Some advocated **Deism**, believing in a creator god who did not intervene in daily affairs. Although many remained formally Catholic, anticlerical sentiment grew, undermining the Church's moral authority. Still, Enlightenment thinkers differed on how far to challenge religion in society. Voltaire famously championed religious freedom but accepted that monarchy and religion could be compatible if reformed.

Reformist Currents at Court

Despite official censorship, some Enlightenment ideas resonated within the monarchy. Louis XV occasionally appointed ministers who recognized the need for administrative or financial reform. Figures like **Turgot** (minister under Louis XVI) were influenced by physiocrats (economic reformers who championed free trade in grain and rational land use). Yet, most attempts at serious reform encountered resistance from parlements and privileged estates, preventing sweeping change and further eroding trust in the old regime's capacity to self-correct.

---

6. The Reign of Louis XVI

Accession of Louis XVI

In 1774, **Louis XVI** inherited the throne at age 19. Polite and well-intentioned, he lacked decisive leadership skills. He was married to **Marie Antoinette**, the daughter of the Austrian empress Maria Theresa—an alliance that made her unpopular among many French, who blamed Austrian influence for France's foreign policy setbacks. Early in his reign, Louis XVI attempted to address pressing financial problems and public discontent.

Ministers and Unsuccessful Reforms

Louis XVI cycled through several finance ministers, each proposing reforms that ran headlong into powerful opposition:

1. **Turgot (1774–1776)**: A disciple of physiocratic thought, he lifted restrictions on grain trade, hoping free markets would promote agricultural efficiency. However, poor harvests led to rising bread prices, triggering the "Flour War" riots. Turgot's proposals to abolish feudal dues and create a fairer tax system also clashed with privileged classes, forcing the king to dismiss him.

2. **Jacques Necker (1777–1781, 1788–1789)**: A Swiss banker who tried to fund state expenses by loans rather than new taxes, hoping to avoid unpopular measures. He published an account of royal finances—*Compte rendu au roi* (1781)—painting a misleadingly optimistic picture. His partial transparency gained him popularity among commoners but sparked hostility from court nobles, and he resigned in 1781. Necker was recalled in 1788, yet the fiscal crisis deepened.
3. **Charles Alexandre de Calonne (1783–1787)**: Proposed a "land tax" that would include privileged estates, plus provincial assemblies to oversee tax collection. The nobility refused to comply, demanding an assembly of notables to discuss finances. This assembly, convened in 1787, rejected Calonne's plan, calling instead for the Estates-General—a meeting of traditional representative bodies—to decide on new taxes. Calonne was dismissed.
4. **Étienne Charles Loménie de Brienne (1787–1788)**: He tried to push similar reforms but faced the same resistance. The Parlement of Paris insisted only the Estates-General could approve new taxes. By 1788, the monarchy hovered on the edge of bankruptcy. Mounting public anger, triggered by economic hardship and contempt for aristocratic privilege, forced Louis XVI to summon the Estates-General in May 1789. This momentous step had not been taken since 1614.

Foreign Policy and the American War of Independence

From 1778 to 1783, France supported the **American colonies** against Britain in the **American War of Independence**, seeing an opportunity to avenge defeats from the Seven Years' War. Though the intervention helped secure American victory, it cost France vast sums of money, worsening the debt. The Treaty of Paris (1783) recognized American independence, marking a diplomatic success for France but providing no immediate financial relief. On the contrary, it heightened the monarchy's monetary woes.

Growing Discontent and Public Opinion

By the late 1780s, all social orders—peasants, bourgeoisie, and even some nobles—criticized the monarchy for mismanaging finances, resisting meaningful reform, and preserving archaic privileges. Bread prices soared when harvests failed. Unemployment rose in cities. The expanding public sphere, fueled by Enlightenment ideas, demanded accountability. Pamphlets attacked Marie Antoinette—derided as "Madame Déficit"—and rumors circulated of lavish spending at Versailles. This stew of anger and hope for change sparked a fervent interest in the upcoming Estates-General, seen as a potential vehicle to fix the kingdom's ills.

---

7. The Estates-General of 1789

Structure of the Estates-General
The Estates-General was a traditional assembly composed of three orders:

1. The **First Estate** (clergy)
2. The **Second Estate** (nobility)
3. The **Third Estate** (commoners—lawyers, merchants, peasants, urban workers)

Historically, each estate voted as a bloc, meaning the First and Second Estates (together representing less than 5% of the population) could outvote the Third Estate (95% of the population). Demands to give the Third Estate more representation or implement "vote by head" were strong but faced resistance from privileged estates.

Cahiers de Doléances (List of Grievances)
In preparation for the Estates-General, communities drafted **cahiers de doléances**, enumerating their complaints and hopes. Common themes included:

- A fairer tax system that would end or reduce noble and clerical exemptions.
- The abolition of feudal dues and corvée labor.
- Greater access to offices and positions for the Third Estate.
- Calls for a constitution limiting arbitrary royal authority, guaranteeing individual rights, and ensuring the Estates-General would meet regularly.

Opening of the Estates-General (May 1789)
On May 5, 1789, Louis XVI opened the Estates-General at Versailles. The atmosphere was charged with expectations. Yet, the old voting system problem quickly paralyzed proceedings. The Third Estate insisted on meeting as a single body with vote by head, while the nobility and much of the clergy opposed it. This impasse fueled frustration and led the Third Estate to take bold steps, eventually proclaiming itself the **National Assembly**, claiming to represent the general will of the nation.

Key Figures
Leaders such as **Emmanuel-Joseph Sieyès**, who wrote the influential pamphlet *What Is the Third Estate?*, insisted that the true strength of the nation lay in the commoners. **Honoré Gabriel Riqueti, Count of Mirabeau**, used his oratory to press for unity and defy attempts by the king's officers to disband the new assembly. Clergymen like **Abbé Grégoire** joined the Third Estate, symbolizing a breach within the First Estate. These events signaled that the old hierarchical order was unraveling under the weight of new ideas and urgent financial crisis.

---

8. Significance of the Late Bourbon Era and Enlightenment Ideas

Intellectual and Cultural Transformation
The Enlightenment profoundly shaped French society, undermining the notion of unquestioned absolute monarchy and widespread religious uniformity. Philosophes introduced critiques of tradition, championing reason and the possibility of reform. Salons, pamphlets, and coffeehouse discussions fostered an informed public eager to debate social and political topics. While not all Enlightenment thinkers advocated a democratic overthrow, their focus on rights, reason, and accountability permeated the Third Estate's demands.

Reform Attempts and Noble Resistance
Repeated efforts by finance ministers to rectify the kingdom's debt and inequitable taxes foundered due to entrenched privilege. Noble parlements framed themselves as defenders of the "rights of the nation," but their real intent was often to maintain their own exemptions. This contradiction—nobles blocking reforms, yet professing to protect the public—alienated many commoners, pushing them to question the entire structure of the Old Regime.

Impending Political Crisis
By 1789, the monarchy's inability to resolve financial and social grievances had reached a breaking point. Rising bread prices, intensifying popular agitation, and the King's halting leadership fed into a revolutionary climate. The convening of the Estates-General offered a chance for orderly reform, but the refusal to accommodate the Third Estate's demands quickly radicalized the situation. Within weeks, Parisian crowds would seize power in key sites, forging a new path for the nation.

Legacy for the French Revolution

The Late Bourbon Era laid the groundwork for revolution. The Enlightenment provided an intellectual arsenal, the financial crisis forced the Crown to seek broad-based changes, and social tensions heightened the call for rights and representation. Even the monarchy's foreign policy mishaps and colonial losses contributed to a sense that absolute rule was ineffective. When the Third Estate declared itself the National Assembly, it was drawing on decades of discontent and new ideas about governance. The stage was set for an upheaval that would transform France and reverberate throughout Europe.

---

9. Conclusion

From the death of Louis XIV in 1715 to the eve of the French Revolution in 1789, France witnessed an evolution in thought, society, and governance. Successive kings—Louis XV and Louis XVI—struggled with mounting debts, social pressures, and calls for reform, yet found themselves unable to reconcile the old structures of privilege with the need for equitable taxation and representation. The Enlightenment, flourishing through salons and printed works, questioned absolute rule, religious orthodoxy, and feudal traditions. Philosophes urged a more rational, humane society, paving the way for demands that the monarchy could no longer ignore.

By 1789, the kingdom was on the brink of a major transformation. Efforts to address the state's financial woes through the Estates-General gave the Third Estate a platform to assert its vision of national sovereignty. Nobles and clergy, clinging to privileges, resisted fundamental changes, inadvertently hastening the collapse of the Old Regime. The tension between these competing visions would explode into revolution—a tumultuous event that would end centuries of Bourbon rule and reshape France forever.

In **Chapter 16**, we will delve into **The French Revolution and the End of the Monarchy**, tracing how the events of 1789 through the early 1790s dismantled the old order. We will see how the National Assembly, popular demonstrations, and radical factions turned a call for reform into a comprehensive reshaping of French society—and, ultimately, the downfall of Louis XVI.

CHAPTER 16: THE FRENCH REVOLUTION AND THE END OF THE MONARCHY

Introduction

In the spring of 1789, the convening of the Estates-General offered hope for peaceful reform in France. Yet within a few months, the country plunged into a **revolution** that dismantled the Old Regime, challenged the foundations of monarchy, and profoundly altered the social and political fabric of Europe. This chapter follows the French Revolution from its outbreak in 1789 to the abolition of the monarchy in 1792 (and the execution of Louis XVI in early 1793), focusing on the swift and dramatic changes that arose once the Third Estate claimed the right to speak for the nation.

Key developments included the creation of the **National Assembly**, the iconic **Storming of the Bastille**, and the sweeping reforms that abolished feudal privileges. The revolution's energies also fueled factional struggles, leading to escalating conflict both inside and outside France. By 1792, foreign invasion threats and internal radicalism prompted the end of the Bourbon monarchy. While these transformations would continue after the king's execution, this chapter ends with the monarchy's downfall, fulfilling the dramatic shift from an absolute ruler to a republic in a matter of a few years.

1. From Estates-General to National Assembly

Voting Controversy
When the Estates-General convened at **Versailles** on May 5, 1789, the long-standing rule dictated that each estate (clergy, nobility, commoners) vote as a separate body. The Third Estate—vastly outnumbering the other two in actual population—demanded a unified assembly with "vote by head." The privileged orders resisted, aiming to preserve their traditional dominance.

After weeks of stalemate, the Third Estate, influenced by pamphlets like Sieyès' *What Is the Third Estate?*, declared itself the **National Assembly** on June 17, 1789. Some liberal-minded clergy joined, signaling a break in the First Estate's unity. The National Assembly claimed it represented the majority of France and thus had the authority to legislate.

Tennis Court Oath

On June 20, the Third Estate's deputies found themselves locked out of their meeting hall. Interpreting this as a royal plot, they gathered instead on an indoor tennis court and swore the **Tennis Court Oath**, vowing not to disband until they drafted a constitution for France. This act of defiance symbolized the shift in sovereignty from the king's authority to the people's representatives. Louis XVI, initially hesitant, recognized the National Assembly under pressure, but tensions escalated as rumors spread of royal troops massing around Paris.

---

2. The Popular Uprising

Storming of the Bastille (July 14, 1789)

Parisians grew alarmed by the arrival of royal regiments near the capital. On July 14, an armed crowd stormed the **Bastille**, an old fortress-prison that symbolized royal despotism. The attackers sought gunpowder and arms, but the fall of the Bastille quickly became a potent revolutionary emblem, proving that popular force could triumph over the monarchy's strongholds. The Bastille's governor was killed, and the building was dismantled.

Impact of Bastille Day

News of the **Storming of the Bastille** electrified the country. Louis XVI recognized the new revolutionary Paris Commune (city government) and withdrew many troops. Lafayette, a hero of the American War of Independence, was appointed commander of the National Guard. This grassroots victory accelerated the revolution's momentum, encouraging peasants and townspeople to take matters into their own hands.

The Great Fear (July–August 1789)

In the countryside, rumors spread that nobles hired brigands to terrorize peasants or seize grain. This paranoia sparked the **Great Fear**, a wave of rural unrest. Peasants attacked manor houses, destroyed feudal records, and sometimes refused to pay dues. Local uprisings forced many nobles to flee or capitulate. The National Assembly responded by seeking to appease these demands in a sweeping act of reform.

3. Abolition of Feudal Privileges and the Declaration of the Rights of Man

August 4 Decrees

Spurred by the Great Fear, on **August 4, 1789**, liberal nobles and clergy in the National Assembly renounced their feudal privileges. They proposed abolishing feudal dues, the tithe to the Church, hunting rights, and all other seigneurial charges. Overnight, centuries of feudal structures were dismantled, as the Assembly passed the **August 4 Decrees**, proclaiming an end to the old social hierarchy. This bold move aimed to quell peasant unrest and unify the nation.

Declaration of the Rights of Man and of the Citizen (August 26, 1789)

Soon after, the Assembly adopted the **Declaration of the Rights of Man and of the Citizen**, a foundational document inspired by Enlightenment ideals and the American Revolution. It asserted principles such as:

1. Men are born free and remain free, with equal rights.
2. The purpose of government is to protect natural rights: liberty, property, security, and resistance to oppression.
3. Sovereignty resides in the nation, not in a single ruler.
4. All citizens are equal before the law and have the right to participate in legislation.

These statements challenged absolute monarchy and noble privilege, establishing a new rhetoric of citizenship. However, the Declaration excluded women from full political rights, indicating the revolution's limits on gender equality (though a few activists like Olympe de Gouges would later question this exclusion).

4. The Women's March on Versailles and the Return of the King to Paris

Economic Hardships and Public Anger
Paris still faced dire bread shortages, as 1789 had been a poor harvest year. High bread prices stirred urban protests. Many ordinary Parisians, especially women responsible for feeding their families, found themselves desperate. Meanwhile, the National Assembly continued debating reforms at Versailles, seemingly disconnected from the daily suffering in the capital.

The Women's March (October 5-6, 1789)
On October 5, a crowd—primarily women—gathered at the Paris city hall demanding bread. They decided to march to Versailles, around 12 miles away, hoping to force the king and the Assembly to address the crisis. Once they arrived, tensions escalated overnight. By the early morning of October 6, some protesters invaded the palace courtyard, clashing with royal guards. The situation grew chaotic. Lafayette and the National Guard intervened, but the crowd demanded that Louis XVI relocate to Paris, where he could see their plight firsthand.

Consequences of the March
Yielding to pressure, Louis XVI and his family left Versailles and moved to the Tuileries Palace in Paris. The National Assembly followed. This transfer of the royal court to the capital symbolized the collapse of the king's aloof authority. From this moment on, the monarchy existed under the watchful eye of the Parisian populace. The revolution's center of gravity also shifted decisively to the city, with popular demonstrations exerting direct influence on the Assembly's decisions.

---

5. Constitutional Monarchy

National Assembly's Ambitious Agenda
Over the next two years, the National Assembly (later renamed the **Constituent Assembly**) worked tirelessly to craft a constitutional framework. Key reforms included:

1. **Administrative Reorganization**: The old provinces, each with unique laws, were replaced by 83 **departements** of roughly equal size. This uniform structure aimed to strengthen national unity and simplify governance.

2. **Judicial Reform**: Feudal courts were abolished. A new system of elected judges emerged, reinforcing the principle of law equal for all.
3. **Ecclesiastical Reforms**: The **Civil Constitution of the Clergy (1790)** nationalized Church lands, making clergy salaried employees of the state and requiring them to swear loyalty to the constitution. This measure alienated many devout Catholics and triggered a schism between "constitutional" clergy who complied and "refractory" clergy who refused.

Debates Over the King's Veto
The Assembly debated the extent of the king's power in the new constitution. Ultimately, they granted Louis XVI a "suspensive veto," enabling him to delay (but not permanently block) legislation. Legislative authority resided chiefly in the elected assembly. Suffrage was restricted to "active citizens" paying a certain tax, excluding many poorer men and all women from voting.

Public Reaction
While these reforms garnered support from liberals and moderate reformers, more radical voices demanded deeper changes, and conservatives worried the revolution had gone too far. The clergy's forced oath caused strife across parishes, undermining revolutionary unity in heavily Catholic regions. Nonetheless, by mid-1791, France stood on the threshold of completing its constitution, hoping the king would accept a limited monarchy.

---

6. The Flight to Varennes and Its Effects

Royal Discontent and Escape Plan
Louis XVI and Marie Antoinette resented their virtual captivity in Paris. Distrusting the revolution, they conspired to flee to the eastern frontier where loyal troops awaited. If successful, they could reestablish absolute rule with foreign help (including Marie Antoinette's Austrian relatives). On the night of June 20, 1791, the royal family disguised themselves and left Paris, hoping to reach Montmédy near the Austrian Netherlands.

Arrest at Varennes
The plan was poorly executed. Recognized en route by a postmaster who had once seen the king's portrait on coins, they were stopped in the town of Varennes. Crowds forced them to return to Paris under armed guard, humiliating the

monarchy. The flight proved the king's insincerity toward constitutional limits, enraging the public and fueling calls for a republic among more radical revolutionaries.

Constitutional Monarchy Undermined
Despite the king's betrayal, moderate deputies still wanted to preserve the monarchy to avoid foreign intervention or civil war. They claimed Louis XVI had been kidnapped, effectively ignoring his own role in the plot. But public trust eroded. Many believed the king could not be trusted to uphold the constitutional order. Political clubs like the **Jacobins** drew more members, some demanding the abolition of kingship altogether.

The flight to Varennes thus marked a turning point, intensifying suspicion of royal collusion with foreign powers. It also sparked a wave of anti-royalist sentiment that would become more pronounced in the coming year.

---

7. Internal Factions and the Growing Radicalization

Political Clubs and Press
As freedoms of speech and assembly expanded, **political clubs** proliferated. Among the most influential were:

1. **Jacobins**: Initially a moderate club, it grew more radical, advocating for a republic. Notable Jacobins included Maximilien Robespierre.
2. **Girondins**: A faction mostly from southwestern regions (the Gironde) that favored a war against foreign monarchies to spread revolutionary ideals and unify France. They still supported a constitutional monarchy but with a more aggressive foreign policy.

Newspapers and pamphlets emerged, fueling debates on every aspect of governance. Journalists like **Jean-Paul Marat** stoked popular anger, especially among the urban poor who demanded relief from high food prices and suspected aristocrats of plotting counterrevolution.

The Legislative Assembly
In October 1791, the newly elected **Legislative Assembly** replaced the National Constituent Assembly. Most original deputies had pledged not to serve in the new legislature, hoping fresh faces would implement the constitution. However, the

Flight to Varennes overshadowed the Assembly's early sessions. Many lawmakers, especially Girondins, pushed for war against Austria, believing conflict would expose traitors at home and rally patriotism.

Declaration of Pillnitz (August 1791)
Foreign monarchs watched events in France with alarm. Emperor Leopold II of Austria (Marie Antoinette's brother) and King Frederick William II of Prussia issued the **Declaration of Pillnitz**, hinting they would intervene if Louis XVI's position was threatened. This statement further radicalized French patriots, convincing them that Europe's crowned heads planned to crush the revolution. Pressures built for a preemptive strike, which the Assembly would authorize by declaring war on Austria in April 1792.

---

8. War, the Fall of the Monarchy, and the Paris Crowd

War with Austria and Prussia
The war declared in April 1792 initially went badly for France. Poorly organized revolutionary armies faced experienced Austrian and Prussian troops. Rumors of treason by royal officers or aristocrats fueled suspicion that the monarchy actively sabotaged the war effort.

Revolutionary Ferment in Paris
In Paris, radical clubs demanded harsher measures against "internal enemies," especially the king. By the summer of 1792, fear of an Austrian-Prussian advance on the capital created a crisis atmosphere. The **Brunswick Manifesto** (July 1792), in which the Prussian commander threatened to punish Paris if any harm befell the royal family, incited outrage. Far from protecting the king, the manifesto emboldened revolutionaries to remove him altogether.

Storming of the Tuileries (August 10, 1792)
On August 10, a large mob backed by provincial militias (the fédérés) attacked the **Tuileries Palace** where Louis XVI resided. The royal Swiss Guards were overwhelmed, and many were killed. The king and his family sought refuge in the Legislative Assembly, which suspended the monarchy's authority and placed the family under arrest. This insurrection effectively ended the constitutional monarchy.

Creation of the National Convention

The Assembly, now dominated by radicals, decreed new elections for a **National Convention** to draft a republican constitution. Universal male suffrage was proclaimed—an unprecedented move. As these events unfolded, Paris erupted in violence. In early September 1792, fearful that imprisoned royalists might join the invading armies, radical mobs carried out the **September Massacres**, killing hundreds of inmates in city prisons. Though horrifying to many, these acts underscored the intensity of revolutionary fervor and the desperation provoked by foreign threats.

---

9. The Trial and Execution of Louis XVI

Proclamation of the Republic
When the **National Convention** convened on September 21, 1792, it abolished the monarchy and declared France a republic. Soon, news arrived that French armies had halted the Prussian advance at the **Battle of Valmy (September 20, 1792)**—a morale boost for revolutionaries. Attention then turned to the fate of the dethroned king, now known as "Citizen Louis Capet."

King on Trial
The Convention put Louis XVI on trial for treason, accusing him of conspiring with foreign powers and opposing the revolution. Secret documents found in the Tuileries seemed to confirm his contacts with Austria and royalist émigrés. Although some moderates favored clemency or exile, radical Jacobins insisted on a death sentence to uphold revolutionary justice. After a tense debate, the Convention voted: a slight majority condemned Louis XVI to death without reprieve.

Execution (January 21, 1793)
On January 21, 1793, Louis XVI was guillotined in Paris. Thousands watched the spectacle. His composure on the scaffold moved some spectators, but the severed head symbolized the irreversible rupture with centuries of Bourbon rule. European monarchies were aghast. The revolution had definitively severed ties to the old order, forging a path to an uncertain future.

CHAPTER 17: THE RISE AND FALL OF NAPOLEON BONAPARTE

Introduction

By 1793, the French Revolution had ended the Old Regime and executed King Louis XVI. Yet the republic that emerged soon found itself entangled in domestic strife and foreign wars, facing coalitions determined to crush revolutionary France. In the midst of this turmoil, a young Corsican artillery officer named **Napoleon Bonaparte** rose through the ranks. Gifted with military brilliance, unrelenting ambition, and a shrewd political sense, Napoleon would dominate the French state from 1799 to 1815, reshaping Europe with both innovative reforms and nearly incessant warfare.

This chapter traces Napoleon's ascendancy from his early military exploits during the **Directory** era to his coup of 18 Brumaire (1799), which established the **Consulate**. We then examine how he crowned himself Emperor, instituted sweeping legal and administrative changes, and fought the **Napoleonic Wars**—a series of conflicts that redrew the map of Europe. The narrative concludes with his dramatic downfall after the disastrous invasion of Russia (1812), the crushing defeats by Allied powers, his abdication, and final exile. Within these eventful years, Napoleon both spread and betrayed some revolutionary ideals, forging a complex legacy that would continue to influence French history long after his exit.

1. France under the Directory

Aftermath of the Terror

Following the **Reign of Terror** under Robespierre and the Committee of Public Safety, France underwent a reaction against radical Jacobinism. Robespierre's overthrow in July 1794 (9 Thermidor) ushered in a more conservative phase. By 1795, the National Convention introduced a new constitution that set up the **Directory**—a five-man executive board—and a bicameral legislature. Suffrage was still limited to property-owning males, and the Directory strove to maintain order against both royalist and neo-Jacobin threats.

Political Instability

Despite attempting to distance itself from the excesses of the Terror, the Directory struggled with widespread corruption, constant factional infighting, and severe economic problems. Food scarcity and inflation persisted, fueling popular discontent. Royalist sympathizers mounted small insurrections, hoping to restore the Bourbon monarchy. Left-wing agitators likewise stirred unrest. The Directory often relied on the army to suppress these uprisings—an approach that gave military officers increasing leverage.

Wars Continue in Europe

France was still at war with several European monarchies, though the revolutionary armies had won significant victories, annexing territories along the Rhine and in the Low Countries. The Directory needed capable generals to safeguard French conquests and push back coalitions forming against the Republic. It was in this context that Napoleon Bonaparte, a general noted for his successes in the Italian campaign, became prominent.

---

2. Napoleon's Early Military Exploits and Rising Fame

Corsican Roots and Revolutionary Beginnings

Born in 1769 on the island of Corsica shortly after its acquisition by France, **Napoleon Bonaparte** came from a minor noble family of modest means. Sent to French military academies, he received an excellent education, excelling in mathematics and artillery tactics. Though Corsica once resisted French rule, Napoleon proved loyal to France, adopting revolutionary ideals in his youth. He rose to public notice by helping recapture the port of Toulon from royalists and British forces in late 1793.

Italian Campaign (1796–1797)

In 1796, the Directory gave Napoleon command of the Army of Italy, then poorly supplied and demoralized. Displaying bold strategy and dynamic leadership, Napoleon rapidly defeated Austrian and Piedmontese forces, pushing them out of

Northern Italy. He reorganized conquered territories into "sister republics" allied to France and compelled Austria to sign the **Treaty of Campo Formio (1797)**, ceding regions in exchange for peace. His dispatches to Paris highlighting the army's exploits made him a national hero. Meanwhile, he cultivated a personal network of loyal officers and administrators, fueling his ambition.

Egyptian Expedition (1798–1799)

Seeking to undermine British trade routes and raise his own prestige, Napoleon proposed an invasion of Egypt. The Directory approved, partly to send away a general grown too popular to manage. In mid-1798, he led a large expeditionary force to Alexandria, rapidly seizing control of the Nile Delta. However, Napoleon's fleet was destroyed by the British Admiral Nelson at the **Battle of the Nile**, cutting off French forces from home. Although the campaign yielded cultural and scientific achievements (the "Egyptian campaign" famously introduced Europe to ancient Egyptian artifacts and produced the **Rosetta Stone** discovery), it became a strategic dead end militarily. By 1799, with the Directory in crisis, Napoleon abandoned his army in Egypt and returned to France, determined to seize power.

---

3. The Coup of 18 Brumaire and the Consulate

Political Context in 1799

Back in France, the Directory was floundering. War with the Second Coalition (Britain, Austria, Russia, the Ottoman Empire) again threatened French gains, and royalist plots were on the rise. Economic troubles persisted. Many believed the government lacked legitimacy and effectiveness. Napoleon's arrival from Egypt was met with relief by moderates who hoped a strong, charismatic figure could stabilize the regime.

The Coup of 18 Brumaire (November 9, 1799)

Working with two Directors—Emmanuel Sieyès and Roger Ducos—Napoleon orchestrated a coup d'état. On 18 Brumaire (Year VIII in the revolutionary calendar), he used troops to dismiss the legislature. Although some lawmakers resisted, Napoleon's supporters prevailed, dissolving the Directory. In its place, they established the **Consulate**, led by three Consuls, with Napoleon as **First Consul**. Sieyès had intended to manipulate Napoleon as a mere figurehead, but the ambitious general quickly outmaneuvered him, taking genuine control.

A New Constitution and Centralized Authority

Under the Constitution of Year VIII, real power rested with Napoleon as First Consul. He held the initiative in legislation, appointed ministers, and commanded the army. While a legislature existed, it had limited authority. Widespread popular support for Napoleon was confirmed through plebiscites that, though not fully free of manipulation, demonstrated the public's exhaustion with chaos and willingness to accept a strong leader. The revolution's core social changes—abolition of feudalism, equal legal status for citizens—remained, but political power was concentrated in the hands of one man.

---

4. Napoleon's Domestic Reforms

Central Administration and the Prefect System

Napoleon reorganized French governance into a highly centralized structure. He instituted the **prefect** system in 1800, naming prefects to oversee each department. These officials answered directly to the central government, enforcing policies uniformly across France and curtailing the independence of local assemblies.

Financial Stabilization and the Bank of France

Napoleon appointed capable administrators like **François de Barbé-Marbois** and **Jean-Baptiste Gaudin** to manage finances. A stable currency was introduced, and in 1800 he founded the **Bank of France**, a private institution with public functions to regulate currency and credit. This ended the monetary chaos of the Revolution, restoring investor confidence. State finances improved, aided by more consistent tax collection and the sale of Louisiana to the United States in 1803 (though primarily done to gain funds for war efforts).

Concordat with the Papacy (1801)

The revolution had left church-state relations in disarray. Napoleon sought reconciliation to bolster social stability. In the **Concordat of 1801**, he recognized Catholicism as the religion of the majority of French citizens (though not the official state religion), while the pope accepted the loss of church lands. The clergy's salaries were paid by the state, and bishops were appointed by Napoleon but confirmed by Rome. This eased religious tensions, though radicals criticized the partial restoration of Catholic influence.

The Napoleonic Code (1804)

Arguably Napoleon's most enduring legacy was the **Civil Code**, later called the Napoleonic Code, promulgated in 1804. It standardized laws across France, guaranteeing equality before the law, protection of property rights, and the secular character of the state. At the same time, it reinforced patriarchal authority within families—husbands had dominant legal power. Women's rights, minimal even under revolutionary legislation, regressed under the Code's strict divorce and property provisions. Still, the Napoleonic Code influenced legal systems far beyond France.

Proclamation as Emperor (1804)

Napoleon's growing authority led him to abandon the title of First Consul for life. In December 1804, he **crowned himself Emperor Napoleon I** in Notre-Dame Cathedral, with Pope Pius VII in attendance. Though critics decried the monarchy's revival, Napoleon argued he was consolidating the Revolution's achievements under a stable imperial regime. A plebiscite again showed popular acquiescence. Thus was born the **First French Empire**, welding revolutionary transformations with monarchical pomp.

---

5. The Napoleonic Wars

Third Coalition and Austerlitz (1805)

Britain, alarmed by Napoleon's ambitions, formed new coalitions on the continent. In 1805, Austria and Russia joined Britain in the **Third Coalition**. Napoleon swiftly marched his Grand Army into Central Europe, delivering a decisive blow at the **Battle of Austerlitz (December 1805)**—sometimes called the "Battle of the Three Emperors," as it involved Napoleon, Emperor Francis II of Austria, and Tsar Alexander I of Russia. The French victory forced Austria to sign the **Treaty of Pressburg**, ceding territory and dismantling the Holy Roman Empire, replaced by the **Confederation of the Rhine** under Napoleon's influence.

Naval Defeat at Trafalgar

While Napoleon triumphed on land, the Royal Navy's victory off the coast of Spain at **Trafalgar (October 1805)** extinguished French hopes of invading Britain. Admiral Nelson's fleet destroyed the Franco-Spanish navy, establishing Britain's naval supremacy for years to come. This defeat pushed Napoleon to seek another method of undermining Britain's economy—namely the **Continental System**.

Continental System

Initiated in 1806 by the **Berlin Decrees**, the Continental System banned European trade with Britain. Napoleon aimed to strangle Britain financially by cutting off its export markets. However, the system proved difficult to enforce, given Britain's control of the seas. Smuggling proliferated, and many European states resented the restrictions, as they relied on British goods. Over time, the blockade inflicted some pain on Britain but also damaged the economies of neutral nations and French allies, sowing discontent.

Battles of Jena-Auerstedt (1806) and Friedland (1807)

Prussia entered the fray, believing it could halt Napoleon's expansion. However, at **Jena and Auerstedt (1806)**, French forces shattered the Prussian army. Next, Napoleon confronted Russia, culminating in the **Battle of Friedland (1807)**, another French victory. Tsar Alexander I agreed to the **Treaties of Tilsit**, effectively dividing Europe between French and Russian spheres of influence. Napoleon reached his zenith, controlling or allying with most continental powers, from Spain to the borders of Russia.

The Peninsular War (1808–1814)

Spain, initially allied to France, became a trap for Napoleon's empire. In 1808, he forced the Spanish king to abdicate and placed his brother, Joseph Bonaparte, on the throne. This provoked a fierce insurgency known as the **Peninsular War**, aided by British troops under Arthur Wellesley (the future Duke of Wellington). Guerrilla warfare and the mountainous terrain tied down hundreds of thousands of French troops. The brutal conflict drained French resources, demonstrating that local resistance could stall Napoleon's mighty armies.

---

6. The Empire's Reorganization and Society under Napoleon

Satellite Kingdoms and Nepotism

Napoleon reorganized Europe to suit his ambitions, creating satellite kingdoms ruled by relatives: Joseph in Spain, Louis in Holland, Jérôme in Westphalia, and others. While these puppet states introduced Napoleonic codes, abolished feudalism, and spurred modernization, they also bred resentment. Local elites bristled at foreign rule, heavy taxation, and conscription for Napoleon's wars.

Nobility of Empire

Though initially a champion of republican ideals, Napoleon restored aristocratic forms. He established a new **Imperial Nobility**, granting titles to generals and officials who demonstrated loyalty and merit in service. This nobility was different from the old Bourbon aristocracy, but it signaled a partial return to hierarchical traditions. While official equality remained in law, social distinctions reemerged in practice.

Economic Policies and Public Works

Napoleon invested in infrastructure, building roads, bridges, and canals. Urban improvements in Paris included the construction of markets and expansions of thoroughfares. A strong central administration oversaw these projects, reflecting the emperor's desire for order and grandeur. However, the Continental System complicated trade, spurring smuggling and creating shortages of some goods. Wealthy merchants found ways around the blockade, but poorer citizens felt the pinch.

Propaganda and Education

Napoleon manipulated public opinion through state-controlled newspapers and bulletins extolling military triumphs. He also modernized the education system by reinforcing **lycées** (secondary schools) to train bureaucrats and soldiers loyal to the regime. Scholarships enabled talented youths from non-elite backgrounds to rise, reflecting a meritocratic ideal, albeit within an authoritarian framework.

---

7. The Invasion of Russia and the Beginning of the End

Friction with Russia

Despite their earlier alliance, relations between Napoleon and Tsar Alexander I deteriorated. Russia's economy suffered under the Continental System, prompting partial defiance. Moreover, the French Empire's expansion into the Grand Duchy of Warsaw alarmed Russia. By 1812, Napoleon resolved to invade Russia to enforce compliance, leading one of history's largest armies—over 500,000 men—into the vast Russian steppes.

The Russian Campaign

Napoleon expected a short, decisive victory, but Russian forces adopted a **scorched-earth** strategy, retreating deeper and burning supplies behind them. Battles like **Borodino (September 1812)** were brutal but inconclusive, costing heavy casualties on both sides. When the French reached Moscow, they found it largely abandoned and then ravaged by fires. Unable to force the Russians to surrender, Napoleon lingered in a ruined city with winter approaching.

The Retreat from Moscow

Facing starvation and freezing temperatures, Napoleon ordered a retreat in October 1812. The grueling march back turned into a catastrophic rout, plagued by Russian raids, snow, and disease. By the time the remnants of the Grand Army crossed the Berezina River in November, tens of thousands had perished, with only a fraction returning to France. This calamity shattered the aura of Napoleon's invincibility.

European Powers Reunite

Sensing Napoleon's vulnerability, Austria, Prussia, and Russia formed a new coalition, joined later by Sweden. Britain supported them financially. The **War of the Sixth Coalition (1813–1814)** aimed to liberate Central Europe from French control. Napoleon hastily raised new armies, but these recruits lacked the seasoned veterans lost in Russia. Key defeats like the **Battle of Leipzig (October 1813)**—known as the "Battle of Nations"—forced French forces to retreat across the Rhine.

8. The First Abdication and the Hundred Days

Allied Invasion of France (1814)

By early 1814, coalition armies converged on French soil. Napoleon launched a skillful defensive campaign, but he was outnumbered. Politically, many of his marshals and ministers urged him to negotiate. Paris fell to the Allies in late March 1814, and Napoleon's empire collapsed. Marshals demanded he abdicate to spare further devastation.

Napoleon initially tried to abdicate in favor of his young son, the "King of Rome," but the Allies insisted on unconditional abdication. **On April 6, 1814,** Napoleon relinquished the throne and accepted exile to the small Mediterranean island of **Elba**, off the Tuscan coast. The victorious Allies restored the Bourbon dynasty in France under **Louis XVIII**, brother of Louis XVI.

The Hundred Days (1815)

Napoleon found life on Elba stifling and saw an opportunity when the restored Bourbon regime in France proved unpopular. In February 1815, he escaped Elba, landed near Cannes, and rallied troops sent to arrest him. Rapidly, Napoleon marched north, regaining supporters who deserted Louis XVIII's cause. This sensational return lasted from March to June 1815, known as the **Hundred Days**. Napoleon entered Paris triumphantly, forcing Louis XVIII to flee.

Despite widespread admiration among the French populace, Europe's powers refused to tolerate his comeback. They swiftly formed the **Seventh Coalition**. Napoleon mobilized for war once more, hoping to defeat the Anglo-Dutch and Prussian armies in Belgium before other forces arrived.

The Battle of Waterloo and Final Exile

On June 18, 1815, Napoleon confronted the Duke of Wellington's Anglo-Dutch forces near the village of **Waterloo**, with the Prussian army under Marshal Blücher approaching. In a grueling battle, Napoleon's attacks were repulsed; the arrival of Prussian reinforcements sealed the French defeat. Routed, Napoleon returned to Paris, where he again abdicated on June 22. Attempting to flee to the United States, he was intercepted by the British and sent into permanent exile on **Saint Helena**, a remote Atlantic island. He died there in 1821, his final ambitions thwarted.

---

9. Legacy of Napoleon and the Napoleonic Age

Revolutionary Ideals and Autocracy

Napoleon both preserved and curtailed the French Revolution's legacy. On one hand, he cemented key principles of the revolution—equality before the law, secular governance, meritocratic advancement—through the Napoleonic Code and administrative reforms. On the other, he reestablished an imperial court, restricted political freedoms, and relied on censorship and propaganda. His autocratic methods revealed that while he championed some modern reforms, he simultaneously embodied a form of personal dictatorship.

French Society Transformed

Under Napoleon, social mobility improved somewhat for talented individuals, especially in the army and bureaucracy. Religious feuds lessened after the Concordat. The old nobility was partially replaced or supplemented by Napoleon's new aristocracy. Feudal vestiges were demolished across large swaths of Europe where French armies marched, spurring modernization in legal and administrative systems beyond France's borders.

Massive Casualties and Warfare Fatigue

Napoleon's continual wars took an enormous toll on human life. Millions of soldiers and civilians perished across Europe. The French population suffered not only in battlefield losses but also from economic disruptions and conscription. Many families bore the cost of extended campaigns in Spain, Germany, Russia, and beyond. By 1815, Europe yearned for peace, prompting a redrawing of frontiers at the **Congress of Vienna**, which sought to contain future French aggression and restore monarchies.

Seeds of Nationalism

Napoleon's occupation of various territories inadvertently ignited **nationalist** sentiments in places like Spain, Germany, and Italy, where locals resented foreign rule and discovered a shared identity in opposing the French. This surge in national consciousness would shape 19th-century revolutions and drive unification movements in Italy and Germany later in the century. Thus, while Napoleon initially conquered large parts of Europe, his actions also led to a backlash that transformed the political landscape.

CHAPTER 18: THE RESTORATION AND THE JULY MONARCHY

Introduction

Napoleon Bonaparte's final defeat at Waterloo (June 1815) paved the way for the **Bourbon Restoration**, a period when the traditional royal dynasty returned to power in France. Despite the monarchy's efforts to reestablish old order, the revolution and the Napoleonic era had irreversibly transformed French society. People had grown accustomed to certain liberties, national representation, and a unified code of laws. Moreover, the notion of absolute divine-right monarchy had lost its former luster.

This chapter explores the Restoration under **Louis XVIII** and **Charles X** (1814–1830), highlighting the tensions between reactionary royalists who yearned for a pre-1789 society and liberals who demanded a constitutional regime. We then examine the **July Revolution of 1830**, which toppled Charles X and installed **Louis-Philippe** of the House of Orléans as a constitutional monarch. This new regime, the **July Monarchy (1830–1848)**, claimed to merge monarchy with the principles of 1789. Yet social and political contradictions persisted, leading to unrest and setting the stage for future revolutions. By tracing these developments, we see how France navigated between restored monarchy and popular movements, searching for equilibrium in the post-Napoleonic world.

1. The First Bourbon Restoration and the Charter of 1814

Louis XVIII's Initial Return (1814–1815)

When Napoleon abdicated in April 1814, the Allied powers placed **Louis XVIII**—brother of Louis XVI—on the French throne. This was known as the **First Restoration**. Louis XVIII, who had lived in exile during the Revolution and Empire, recognized the need for compromise. Europe had changed too dramatically for a pure return to absolute rule. Instead, he issued the **Charter of 1814**, a constitutional document granting certain rights while preserving a degree of royal authority.

The Charter of 1814

The charter declared:

1. **Bicameral Legislature**: A Chamber of Peers (appointed by the king) and a Chamber of Deputies (elected under a restricted franchise favoring property owners).
2. **Civil Equality and Napoleonic Institutions**: It upheld the Napoleonic Code, maintained administrative divisions, and recognized freedom of religion.
3. **Royal Prerogatives**: The king retained power over foreign policy, the military, and legislative initiatives, though laws required legislative approval.

By preserving many revolutionary and Napoleonic reforms, Louis XVIII hoped to reconcile moderate liberals to the Bourbon monarchy. Royalists who desired a full rollback of 1789 felt disappointed, but the Allies demanded a stable constitutional monarchy as part of postwar settlements.

The Hundred Days Interruption

Before this Restoration could solidify, Napoleon returned from Elba in February 1815, briefly dethroning Louis XVIII. This "Hundred Days" ended after Waterloo, and Louis XVIII re-entered Paris in July 1815 under Allied escort. The so-called **Second Restoration** then commenced. Distrustful of liberal gains, Ultra-royalists demanded vengeance on those who had supported Napoleon or the Revolution, foreshadowing more divisive politics.

---

2. The Second Restoration and the White Terror

Ultra-Royalist Reaction

Upon regaining power after Waterloo, the monarchy faced two main political blocs:

- **Ultras**: Extreme royalists who demanded harsh measures against "traitors" (regicides, Bonapartists, and liberal revolutionaries).
- **Moderate Royalists and Liberals**: Favored a reconciliation policy, respecting many changes since 1789.

In the climate of fear and revenge, the **Ultras** briefly dominated. They instigated the **White Terror** (1815–1816), targeting former revolutionaries and imperial officials. Vigilante mobs and occasional official proceedings led to executions or exile of suspected Bonapartists.

Role of Allied Occupation

Allied armies occupied parts of France to ensure indemnities were paid and to guarantee no further Napoleonic resurgence. This external pressure forced Louis XVIII to balance appeasing the Ultras with avoiding internal revolt or renewed coalition wrath. Over time, the Allies withdrew as France complied with treaties and war indemnities, though lingering resentment of the monarchy's reliance on foreign arms remained.

Moderation Under Louis XVIII

Gradually, Louis XVIII and more moderate ministers, such as **Élie Decazes**, curbed the Ultras' extremism. In 1816, the king dissolved an ultra-royalist Chamber of Deputies, replacing it with a more balanced assembly. This shift sought to stabilize the regime. However, tensions persisted between Ultras who wanted a full pre-1789 restoration and liberals insisting on constitutional freedoms. By 1820, events would again tip the balance in favor of reactionary forces.

---

3. The Assassination of the Duke of Berry and the Rise of Charles X

Succession Concerns

Louis XVIII had no direct heirs, and the future of the Bourbon line depended on his brother, the **Count of Artois** (the future Charles X), and the Duke of Berry, Artois's son. In February 1820, a Bonapartist sympathizer assassinated the Duke of Berry, robbing the Bourbons of a key young heir. However, Berry's widow was pregnant; a posthumous son (the future Count of Chambord) was born later in 1820. Nonetheless, the assassination fueled fear of revolutionary plots, strengthening reactionary demands.

Politicization of the Tragedy

Shocked by the Duke of Berry's murder, Ultras blamed liberalism for spawning violent conspiracies. They called for stricter censorship and increased police powers. Louis XVIII, aging and more cautious, allowed his ministers to pass **repressive laws** that curtailed freedom of the press and assembly, hoping to forestall unrest. Many liberals objected, but the monarchy cast the policies as necessary for public safety.

Charles X Ascends (1824)

Louis XVIII died in 1824, succeeded by his brother, the Count of Artois, who took the throne as **Charles X**. Known for his ultra-royalist sympathies since the revolution's early days, Charles X sought to fully reassert traditional monarchy and Catholic influence. His coronation in Reims revived ancient ceremonies reminiscent of the pre-revolutionary era, disquieting liberals who saw these displays as a step backward.

---

4. Charles X's Ultra-Royalist Reign and Growing Opposition

The Return to Conservatism

Charles X governed with a circle of ultra-royalist ministers like **Jean-Baptiste de Villèle** (until 1828), championing clerical power and aristocratic privileges. Some key policies included:

1. **Indemnities for Émigrés**: Large financial compensation to nobles who lost property during the revolution.
2. **Religious Education**: Greater Church control over schools, reversing some Napoleonic-era secularism.
3. **Censorship**: Reinforced press restrictions, punishing editors who criticized the monarchy.

These measures angered the expanding liberal middle class, who believed constitutional guarantees were being eroded. Many lower nobility and bourgeoisie resented paying taxes to fund émigré indemnities. Furthermore, there was limited tolerance for dissent, fueling a sense that the regime was turning back the clock to the Old Regime.

Liberal Resistance

By the late 1820s, liberal intellectuals like **Benjamin Constant** and **François Guizot** criticized Charles X's government in newspapers and pamphlets, calling for a truly parliamentary monarchy with accountable ministers. The Chamber of Deputies featured a growing bloc of liberal deputies who demanded more representation for the rising bourgeois class. Economic growth from industrial and colonial ventures in Algeria (which France began conquering in 1830) produced a wealthier middle class that felt marginalized by the ultra-royalist regime.

Polignac Ministry and the Final Crisis

After a short period of moderate governance under **Jean-Baptiste de Martignac**, Charles X appointed the ultra-royalist **Jules de Polignac** as head of government in 1829. Polignac's reactionary stance antagonized the already restive liberal deputies. The king soon confronted a hostile Chamber that refused to ratify new taxes or policies. Charles X, convinced of his divine right, decided to overrule parliament by royal decree. This confrontation would spark the final crisis of his reign.

---

5. The July Revolution of 1830

The Four Ordinances

On July 25, 1830, Charles X issued the **Four Ordinances** (also called the **Ordinances of Saint-Cloud**). These decrees:

1. Suspended freedom of the press.
2. Dissolved the recently elected Chamber of Deputies (dominated by liberals).
3. Reduced the electorate significantly by raising property qualifications for voting.
4. Called for new elections under these restrictive conditions.

These ordinances brazenly violated the Charter of 1814, effectively dismantling constitutional government. Outrage rippled through Paris, with liberal journalists (including **Adolphe Thiers**) calling for resistance.

Uprising in Paris (July 27–29, 1830)

Within days, barricades appeared in the streets. Students, artisans, and workers clashed with the royal troops. Despite limited arms, the Parisians managed to seize control of the capital. Soldiers, many sympathetic to liberal causes, hesitated to use force, especially since the monarchy's popularity had plummeted. By July 29, the Hôtel de Ville (City Hall) was in revolutionary hands, and the king's authority in Paris collapsed.

Abdication of Charles X

Facing the impossible, Charles X abdicated on August 2, 1830, in favor of his grandson, the young Duke of Bordeaux. However, liberal leaders in Paris refused to accept another Bourbon. Instead, they offered the crown to **Louis-Philippe**, Duke of Orléans, a relative of the Bourbon line but known for his more liberal sympathies. With support from bankers like **Jacques Laffitte** and influential politicians, Louis-Philippe assumed power as a **"Citizen King."**

---

6. The July Monarchy under Louis-Philippe

A "Bourgeois Monarchy"

Louis-Philippe took the title "King of the French" rather than "King of France," suggesting a contract with the nation rather than a divine right. He adopted modest attire and walked the streets with minimal ceremony. Nevertheless, real power remained largely in the hands of property-owning elites. The new regime revised the Charter, reaffirming many liberties:

1. Press freedoms were somewhat expanded.
2. The franchise was broadened—but still limited to the wealthier classes.
3. Roman Catholicism was no longer the official state religion, but recognized as the religion of most citizens.

While these changes satisfied some liberals, left-wing republicans felt the new monarchy had not gone far enough, and ultra-royalists despised it as an illegitimate usurpation.

Political Divisions under the July Monarchy

Louis-Philippe's regime included a range of parliamentary factions:

- **Doctrinaires**: Moderates like François Guizot, who believed in a constitutional monarchy with a narrow franchise.

- **Orleanist Liberals**: Supported the new monarchy but pressed for incremental reforms.
- **Republicans**: Sought universal male suffrage and an end to monarchy altogether. They were often suppressed by government crackdowns.
- **Legitimists**: Royalists loyal to Charles X's line, regarding Louis-Philippe as a usurper, waiting for the Count of Chambord (the exiled Bourbon heir) to reclaim the throne.

This fragmented political environment witnessed frequent ministerial changes. While the king worked with parliamentary majorities, he also exercised considerable personal influence, resisting expansions of the electorate. Social tensions simmered, especially as industrialization advanced, creating new labor disputes.

Economic Developments

The 1830s and 1840s saw the growth of railways, coal mining, and textiles in regions like northern France, Alsace, and the Loire. A new industrial bourgeoisie emerged, pressing for policies that favored commerce. Meanwhile, workers in urban centers faced low wages, poor working conditions, and lack of political representation, leading to occasional strikes or riots. The monarchy's reluctance to address social grievances steadily eroded its legitimacy among the lower classes.

Foreign Policy

Louis-Philippe's government adopted a cautious stance abroad, shaped by Foreign Minister **François Guizot** in the 1840s. While Britain remained a key partner, tensions arose over colonial expansions. In 1830, soon after seizing power, the new regime inherited the **Algerian conquest**, begun by Charles X. Over the next decades, French control in Algeria expanded, though at the cost of brutal conflicts with local populations. The monarchy's policy in Europe, meanwhile, tried to balance alliances without entangling France in major wars, mindful of the traumatic Napoleonic legacy. That said, national pride demanded some diplomatic successes, such as limited interventions in Belgium's independence from the Netherlands (1830–1831) and the management of crises in the eastern Mediterranean.

7. Social Discontent and the Rise of Opposition Movements

Republican Agitation

Despite the monarchy's moderate-liberal veneer, genuine republicans felt betrayed. Secret societies formed, reminiscent of earlier revolutionary clubs. Several insurrections erupted, notably in 1832 and 1834, often in Paris or Lyons, where workers rose in protest. The regime brutally suppressed these uprisings. While these attempts failed, they revealed deep discontent among the lower classes and radical intellectuals.

Worker Revolts

Industrialization caused wage labor to increase in urban centers. Craftsmen and factory workers faced uncertain employment, low pay, and harsh conditions. The famous **Lyons Silk Weavers' Revolts** of 1831 and 1834 (the "Canut revolts") demanded a living wage and better conditions, but the government responded with force. These episodes of social unrest demonstrated that the new monarchy could be as repressive as the old when confronting popular demands.

The Banquet Campaign and Reform Movement

By the late 1840s, a coalition of moderate liberals, journalists, and opposition deputies championed broader suffrage and political reform. The existing property-based voter qualifications enfranchised only around 1% of the population, fueling cries for **"electoral reform."** As the king and his conservative cabinet (dominated by Guizot) resisted any serious expansion of the electorate, reformists organized "banquets"—public gatherings where speakers promoted democratic ideas without officially violating assembly laws. These banquets grew increasingly popular, alarming the regime.

---

8. The End of the July Monarchy and Prelude to Future Changes

Economic Downturn

In 1846–1847, an economic crisis hit Europe, triggered by poor harvests and the Irish potato famine. In France, grain prices soared, wages stagnated, and financial

176

scandals involving government ministers eroded public trust. Political corruption and rising unemployment further embittered the urban population.

The February Revolution (1848)

When the government banned a large reform banquet in Paris scheduled for February 22, 1848, crowds protested, calling for Guizot's resignation and demanding universal male suffrage. Over two days of unrest, barricades appeared again in Paris. Guizot resigned, and Louis-Philippe, hoping to calm the situation, appointed a more liberal cabinet. But the protests continued, culminating on February 24 with the king's abdication. Lacking broad support and fearing a repeat of the 1830 scenario, Louis-Philippe fled to Britain under disguise.

Establishment of the Second Republic

Immediately after Louis-Philippe's flight, revolutionaries proclaimed a provisional government, marking the **end of the July Monarchy** and the birth of the **Second Republic**. This new government quickly introduced universal male suffrage, declared freedoms of assembly and press, and promised social reforms. France once again entered a republican phase, albeit uncertain and beset by divisions between moderates and socialists.

---

9. Significance of the Restoration and the July Monarchy

Oscillation Between Tradition and Reform

The Bourbon Restoration and the July Monarchy revealed France's struggle to reconcile monarchical traditions with revolutionary ideals. Louis XVIII's Charter of 1814 recognized many Napoleonic and revolutionary changes, but Ultra-royalists under Charles X attempted to restore pre-1789 social and religious structures. This clash inevitably led to the July Revolution. Louis-Philippe then sought a "juste milieu" (middle way) monarchy, but ultimately failed to satisfy either the conservative aristocracy or a growing liberal and working-class constituency demanding deeper reforms.

Constitutional Experiments

Both regimes—the Restoration (with its Charter) and the July Monarchy—experimented with constitutional governance. A parliament existed, but suffrage remained narrow, and the king retained broad executive powers. Although these structures advanced beyond absolute monarchy, they fell short of a true parliamentary democracy. Repeated showdowns between royal prerogatives and elected chambers indicated a profound desire for more inclusive politics.

Social Shifts and the Rise of the Bourgeoisie

The Restoration and July Monarchy saw the consolidation of a bourgeois elite—wealthy businessmen, bankers, merchants—who gained political influence through restricted franchises. Yet, industrial growth also generated a new working class that lacked political representation, fueling labor unrest. The monarchy's alliance with the upper bourgeoisie shaped policy, intensifying dissatisfaction among peasants burdened by taxes, artisans threatened by industrial changes, and intellectuals yearning for liberal reforms.

Path to 1848 and the Second Republic

By 1848, France was ripe for another upheaval. Economic crises, refusal to broaden suffrage, and continued corruption in high places undermined the monarchy's credibility. The revolution of February 1848 was thus not an isolated event but the culmination of decades-long pressures for more democratic representation and social justice. It toppled Louis-Philippe, demonstrating once again that partial reforms and suppressed dissent could not permanently contain the legacy of 1789.

CHAPTER 19: THE SECOND EMPIRE AND THE RISE OF NATIONALISM

Introduction

The Revolution of 1848 toppled the July Monarchy, establishing the Second Republic under a provisional government. It introduced universal male suffrage and briefly raised hopes for a genuinely democratic and socially responsive regime. Yet, political and economic challenges soon tested the Republic. Into this volatile setting stepped **Louis-Napoleon Bonaparte**, nephew of the famous Emperor Napoleon I. A canny politician, Louis-Napoleon leveraged widespread nostalgia for the Napoleonic legend, appealing to peasants, workers, and conservatives alike.

Elected President in December 1848, Louis-Napoleon systematically concentrated power, ultimately carrying out a coup d'état in December 1851. By late 1852, he had proclaimed himself **Napoleon III**, Emperor of the French, inaugurating the **Second Empire (1852–1870)**. This chapter examines how Napoleon III combined authoritarian rule with economic modernization, how he nurtured a nationalist spirit at home, and how his foreign ventures—particularly the Crimean War, adventures in Italy, and interventions beyond Europe—shaped France's trajectory. We will also analyze the empire's downfall, triggered by the disastrous Franco-Prussian War (1870–1871), and the broader rise of nationalism that transformed European politics in the mid- to late-19th century.

1. The Second Republic

Provisional Government and Early Reforms

After the February Revolution of 1848 ousted Louis-Philippe, a provisional government declared the **Second Republic**. It introduced:

1. **Universal Male Suffrage**: Over eight million Frenchmen could now vote, a radical leap from the narrow property-based system of the July Monarchy.

2. **Social Measures**: Bowing to pressure from workers, the government set up **National Workshops** to provide jobs. The influential socialist Louis Blanc proposed these workshops, hoping to reduce unemployment and alleviate urban poverty.

Initial optimism, however, soon collided with fiscal reality. The cost of the National Workshops strained state finances, and bourgeois politicians worried about radicalism among the urban poor. Tensions between moderate republicans and socialist factions deepened.

June Days Uprising (1848)

When the provisional government closed the National Workshops in June 1848, thousands of workers in Paris revolted. Over several days (June 23–26), barricades reappeared, and the uprising was brutally crushed by General Cavaignac's forces. The **June Days** marked a decisive defeat for the revolutionary left, alienating many workers from the moderate republic. This event also heightened the public's longing for order and stability, paving the way for Louis-Napoleon Bonaparte's rise.

Presidential Election and Louis-Napoleon's Triumph

In December 1848, France held its first direct presidential election. Louis-Napoleon Bonaparte leveraged his family name, promising to reconcile social classes and restore French grandeur. His message resonated with peasants seeking stability, urban workers recalling the Napoleonic legend, and conservatives fearing renewed radical turmoil. He won an overwhelming majority (over 70% of the vote). Over the next three years, he consolidated influence, cultivating an image of paternal benevolence while maneuvering to extend his term beyond the constitutional limit of four years.

---

2. The Coup of 1851 and the Proclamation of the Second Empire

Political Maneuvering

The 1848 Constitution barred a president from immediate re-election. Facing the end of his term in 1852, Louis-Napoleon pressed the National Assembly to amend the constitution. When they refused, he orchestrated a **coup d'état** on December 2,

1851—symbolically the anniversary of Napoleon I's coronation and the victory at Austerlitz. Troops loyal to him dissolved the Assembly, arrested key opponents, and staged a plebiscite that endorsed his seizure of power.

Consolidation of Authority

Following the coup, Louis-Napoleon ruled as an authoritarian leader, tightening censorship and exiling or jailing thousands of republicans. Another plebiscite in late 1852 overwhelmingly approved the revival of the imperial title. On December 2, 1852, he proclaimed himself **Emperor Napoleon III**. Official propaganda depicted him as the guardian of universal suffrage, social progress, and national unity—though the regime in practice restricted civil liberties and concentrated power in the emperor's hands.

The Constitution of 1852

Under the new imperial constitution:

1. **Executive Power**: The emperor controlled the government, appointed ministers, and could propose or dismiss legislation.
2. **Legislative Bodies**: The Corps Législatif (legislature) was elected by universal male suffrage, but it had limited powers. A second body, the Senate, was handpicked by Napoleon III.
3. **Plebiscites**: Napoleon III frequently used referendums to claim popular legitimacy. Voting was often influenced by government pressure and manipulated by official propaganda.

While critics saw the Second Empire as a personal dictatorship, Napoleon III insisted it reconciled monarchy with democratic principles, claiming to champion the popular will. Over time, the empire's authoritarian character would soften, moving toward a "liberal empire" in the 1860s.

---

3. Domestic Policies and Economic Modernization

Haussmann's Renovation of Paris

One of Napoleon III's most famous undertakings was the transformation of **Paris** under the direction of Baron **Georges-Eugène Haussmann**. From the 1850s through the 1860s, medieval neighborhoods were cleared, replaced by wide boulevards, grand avenues, parks, and modern sewers. The goals included:

1. **Public Health**: New boulevards and improved sanitation reduced disease and overcrowding.
2. **Urban Aesthetics**: Napoleon III aimed to make Paris the showcase capital of Europe, reflecting the empire's grandeur.
3. **Security**: Wide boulevards facilitated troop movement and reduced the effectiveness of barricades—lessons drawn from 1848.

Though controversial—thousands of working-class residents were displaced—the Haussmann plan profoundly shaped modern Paris, with iconic boulevards like the Avenue de l'Opéra and expansions of green spaces (e.g., the Bois de Boulogne).

Industrial and Financial Growth

Napoleon III promoted infrastructure projects, including:

- **Railroad Expansion**: The empire encouraged private investment in rail lines, binding regional markets together and stimulating heavy industry. Cities like Lille and Lyon benefited from better connections to Paris, boosting trade.
- **Banking and Credit**: New credit institutions, such as Crédit Mobilier, financed large-scale industrial ventures. The state also supported the creation of savings banks for small depositors.
- **Free Trade Policies**: In a bold departure from protectionism, Napoleon III signed a **free trade treaty with Britain (1860)**. While it lowered tariffs on many goods, spurring competition and cheaper consumer prices, French manufacturers sometimes struggled against British industrial dominance. These moves exemplified his attempt to merge social welfare (affordable goods) with economic liberalization.

Social Welfare Initiatives

The emperor occasionally adopted paternalistic social reforms to bolster his support among workers. For instance, he legalized workers' mutual aid societies and recognized the right of workers to form limited associations. However, strikes remained subject to police crackdowns, and full labor union rights were not established. The regime thus sought to placate the urban working class without granting them robust political influence.

4. Foreign Policy and Adventurism under Napoleon III

The Crimean War (1853–1856)

Napoleon III aspired to restore France's stature as a leading power. In the **Crimean War**, France allied with Britain and the Ottoman Empire against Russia, ostensibly to defend Christian minorities and limit Russian expansion. The war, fought largely in the Black Sea region, featured famous engagements like the Siege of Sevastopol. Victory in 1856 at the Peace of Paris gave Napoleon III prestige, though the conflict's strategic gains were modest. Still, it signaled that France had re-emerged as a major force, overturning the Vienna settlement from post-1815.

Italian Unification and France's Role

Napoleon III held ambiguous views on Italian unification, partly shaped by his youth in exile and sympathy for nationalist movements, but also by dynastic and Catholic considerations. In 1859, he allied with **Piedmont-Sardinia** to drive Austrian influence out of northern Italy, hoping to reshape the peninsula under friendly regimes. Key battles at **Magenta** and **Solferino** ended in Austrian defeats. By the **Treaty of Villafranca (1859)**, Austria ceded Lombardy to Piedmont, while France received **Nice and Savoy** as compensation. However, further unification in central and southern Italy largely proceeded without French leadership, culminating in the Kingdom of Italy (1861). Although Napoleon III gained territory, Catholic conservatives criticized him for undermining the pope's temporal power. Meanwhile, Italian nationalists felt betrayed by his partial deals.

Mexico Expedition (1862–1867)

One of Napoleon III's more ill-fated ventures was the attempt to install a pro-French monarchy in Mexico under **Archduke Maximilian of Austria**. In 1862, French troops intervened, initially routing Mexican forces. However, local resistance, led by President Benito Juárez, intensified. The French endured guerrilla warfare and American diplomatic pressure (especially after the U.S. Civil War ended). Ultimately, the venture collapsed in 1867. Maximilian was executed, and France withdrew in disgrace. The fiasco tarnished Napoleon III's image abroad and revealed the limits of imperial adventures outside Europe.

Growing Rivalry with Prussia

In the 1860s, **Prussia**—under Chancellor Otto von Bismarck—rose as a formidable German power, defeating Denmark (1864) and Austria (1866). Napoleon III attempted to maneuver diplomatically, underestimating Bismarck's strategic cunning. The creation of the North German Confederation in 1867 alarmed France, which feared being encircled by a strong, unified German state. Franco-Prussian tensions simmered, culminating in a final confrontation that would topple the Second Empire.

---

5. Political Liberalization and the Collapse of the Second Empire

The "Liberal Empire" Reforms

From around 1860, domestic opposition to the empire's authoritarian structure gradually increased. Republicans, Orléanist monarchists, and liberal Catholics criticized censorship and the limited powers of the legislative body. Under pressure, Napoleon III introduced liberalizing measures, such as:

1. **Relaxed Censorship**: Newspapers gained more freedom to criticize government policies.
2. **Legislative Powers**: The Corps Législatif received the right to debate and propose amendments on laws.
3. **Ministerial Responsibility**: In 1870, the emperor granted the legislature a say in ministerial appointments, edging toward a parliamentary monarchy.

Though these reforms appeased some liberals, they also emboldened critics to demand deeper change. Amid economic challenges and foreign policy setbacks, public confidence in the regime waned.

Franco-Prussian War (1870–1871)

The immediate spark of war came with the **Ems Dispatch** (July 1870), manipulated by Bismarck to incite French outrage over a Hohenzollern candidacy for the Spanish throne. Napoleon III declared war on Prussia, hoping to rally national pride and secure a quick victory. However:

- **Military Unpreparedness**: The French army was poorly organized, lacking modern staff coordination. Superior Prussian mobilization and technology (e.g., breech-loading rifles) quickly tilted the balance.
- **Key Defeats**: Early French reverses culminated in the catastrophic surrender at **Sedan (September 2, 1870)**, where Napoleon III himself was captured. This humiliation triggered an uprising in Paris that proclaimed the end of the Empire.
- **Occupation and Siege of Paris**: German forces encircled the capital, enduring a prolonged siege until January 1871.

With Napoleon III a prisoner of war, the Second Empire crumbled. Bismarck declared the German Empire in the Hall of Mirrors at Versailles (January 1871), while a provisional government in France strove to negotiate peace, concluding the **Treaty of Frankfurt (May 1871)**, ceding Alsace and part of Lorraine to the new German Empire. This national trauma left deep scars on French consciousness, fueling revanchist sentiments that shaped future Franco-German relations.

---

6. The Rise of Nationalism and the Broader European Context

Unification of Italy and Germany

During Napoleon III's reign, Europe saw the dramatic unification of Italy and Germany—processes that Napoleon's interventions (in Italy) or miscalculations (vis-à-vis Prussia) indirectly spurred. These national unifications revealed the potency of nationalist sentiment and modern state-building. The old multinational empires, like Austria's Habsburg realm, struggled against these dynamic forces, leading to significant redrawing of Europe's political map.

Impact on France

France's defeat in the Franco-Prussian War shattered illusions of military supremacy. The loss of Alsace-Lorraine was seen as a national humiliation, fueling calls for revenge ("revanchisme"). National identity sharpened; many French people blamed the monarchy or imperial regime for the catastrophe. This crisis of identity would shape the early Third Republic, with a new wave of patriotic fervor, universal conscription, and educational reforms designed to strengthen the sense of Frenchness.

Emergence of Mass Politics

Across Europe, the mid- to late-19th century saw an expansion of political participation and the growth of mass movements. In France, the universal male suffrage introduced in 1848 persisted under the Second Empire but was carefully managed. By the war's end, new political clubs, socialist groups, and radical republicans demanded a voice in post-war reconstruction. The subsequent government would have to balance these pressures amid the ongoing heartbreak of defeat.

---

7. The Legacy of Napoleon III and the Second Empire

Achievements and Contradictions

Napoleon III's rule combined modernizing impulses—economic growth, urban renewal, public works, liberalizing concessions in the 1860s—with an authoritarian foundation that suppressed opposition for much of his reign. The empire's first decade especially saw prosperity and infrastructural leaps, but reliance on personal power, propaganda, and foreign exploits proved unsustainable.

At home, the transformation of Paris remains one of his most visible legacies, symbolizing both civic improvement and top-down control. Abroad, his initial diplomatic successes eventually gave way to miscalculations that led France into a calamitous war with Prussia. Napoleon III himself, captive after Sedan, was allowed to go into exile in England, where he died in 1873, overshadowed by the catastrophic end of his empire.

Shaping Modern French Nationalism

The Second Empire's downfall and loss of Alsace-Lorraine catalyzed a fervent strain of nationalism in France. Intellectuals, politicians, and veterans alike swore that future generations would rectify this "mutilation" of the homeland. Meanwhile, the political vacuum left by the empire's collapse enabled the birth of the Third Republic (1870), which, after overcoming internal conflicts (notably the Paris Commune), outlasted earlier experiments in monarchy and empire.

The memory of Napoleonic glory lingered, inspiring certain Bonapartist circles, but the decisive Prussian victory ended illusions that personal leadership alone could guarantee success. Instead, France would increasingly emphasize civic institutions, professionalized armies, and broad-based political engagement—lessons drawn from the failures of 1870.

---

8. Conclusion

Between the overthrow of the July Monarchy in 1848 and the fall of the Second Empire in 1870, France traversed an eventful path marked by republican aspirations, an authoritarian imperial regime, and significant foreign entanglements. The presidency and subsequent empire of **Louis-Napoleon Bonaparte**—Napoleon III—offered stability and modernization at first but concluded in disastrous defeat at the hands of a newly unified Germany. Domestically, the Second Empire profoundly reshaped France's economy, infrastructure, and society, leaving a complex legacy of progress tempered by lost liberties.

The swirling forces of **nationalism** also profoundly reshaped Europe during this period. Napoleon III's interventions in Italy aided the cause of unification, while his miscalculated war with Prussia accelerated Germany's formation under Bismarck. For France, the humiliation of 1870–1871 would spark a new wave of patriotic reorganization under the **Third Republic**, forging a state that—despite internal turbulence—would endure into the early 20th century.

In **Chapter 20**, we turn to **The Third Republic and France at the End of the 19th Century**, examining how France rebuilt itself post-Franco-Prussian War, navigated internal political crises (such as the Paris Commune and the Dreyfus Affair), and established a republican regime that proved surprisingly resilient, shaping the nation's political culture leading into the 20th century.

CHAPTER 20: THE THIRD REPUBLIC AND FRANCE AT THE END OF THE 19TH CENTURY

Introduction

The collapse of the Second Empire in 1870 ushered in a new era in French history: the **Third Republic** (1870–1940). Born of a humiliating defeat to Prussia, it faced an immediate crisis—the Siege of Paris, the Paris Commune uprising, and negotiations with the new German Empire. Despite these tumultuous beginnings, the Third Republic gradually established itself as the longest-lasting regime in France since the 1789 Revolution. It introduced robust civic institutions, expanded public education, and grappled with ideological challenges ranging from monarchist plots to republican divisions and the rising forces of socialism.

In this final chapter, we will examine the early years of the Third Republic, including the **Paris Commune (1871)** and the forging of a constitutional framework. We will explore how republican leaders overcame royalist attempts to restore the monarchy and consolidated republican values through free schooling, secular policies, and symbolic gestures like the national anthem and the tricolor flag. Finally, we delve into the major social and political crises of the late 19th century, culminating in the **Dreyfus Affair**, which tested the Republic's commitment to justice and ultimately reinforced republican principles. By the end of the 19th century, France stood as a parliamentary democracy with a strong sense of secular national identity, setting the stage for the challenges of the 20th century (beyond our scope here).

1. The Immediate Aftermath of Franco-Prussian War

Siege of Paris and Armistice

The **Government of National Defense**, formed in September 1870 after Napoleon III's capture, attempted to rally French forces against the Prussian invasion. Paris endured a **siege** (September 1870–January 1871), marked by severe food shortages. Despite valiant balloon flights delivering messages and sporadic attempts at breakout, the capital eventually capitulated. An armistice followed, leading to the **Treaty of Frankfurt (May 1871)**, which forced France to cede **Alsace** and part of **Lorraine**, pay a massive indemnity, and endure temporary German occupation in eastern departments.

Outrage and Emergence of the Commune

Many Parisians felt betrayed by the conservative national assembly that sought a quick peace with Prussia. In March 1871, tensions exploded when the government under Adolphe Thiers tried to disarm the **National Guard** in Paris. Citizens refused, forming an autonomous municipal government, the **Paris Commune (March–May 1871)**. The Commune espoused revolutionary ideals—workers' rights, secular governance, direct democracy—and distanced itself from the national assembly in Versailles.

Bloody Suppression

Thiers's government, backed by French regular troops, besieged Paris once more. In late May 1871, army units stormed the city, crushing the Commune in a week of brutal street fighting known as the **Semaine Sanglante (Bloody Week)**. Thousands of communards died or were deported. This internal conflict left deep scars. Conservatives and moderates condemned the Commune as anarchy, while leftist movements revered it as a heroic stand for social justice. Although short-lived, the Commune influenced future socialist and Marxist thought worldwide.

---

2. Founding the Third Republic

The 1871 Assembly and Monarchist Majority

Elections for a new National Assembly in February 1871 yielded a conservative majority, including many monarchists—Legitimists (supporters of the Bourbon line) and Orléanists (followers of the House of Orléans). The assembly installed **Adolphe Thiers** as "Chief of the Executive Power," effectively head of state. Initially, it seemed monarchy might be restored, as the Franco-Prussian War had discredited the Bonapartist empire, and republican forces were weakened by the Commune's defeat.

However, divisions among monarchists—particularly between Legitimists loyal to the Count of Chambord (Henry V) and Orléanists favoring the Comte de Paris—blocked a consensus restoration. The Count of Chambord refused to accept the tricolor flag, insisting on the Bourbon white flag. This symbolic dispute proved insurmountable.

Thiers's Role and Resignation

Thiers, though initially a moderate conservative, recognized that public opinion, especially in urban areas, opposed a Bourbon monarchy. He moved toward republican policies, working to repay the German indemnity swiftly and prompting the withdrawal of occupying troops by 1873. When monarchists realized Thiers was no longer an ally for restoration, they forced him to resign. The assembly replaced him with **Marshal Patrice de MacMahon**, a devout Catholic and royalist sympathizer, as President.

The Failure of Monarchical Restoration

Despite MacMahon's presidency, the Bourbon claimant's intransigence (refusing the tricolor) made restoration impossible. As the years passed, the assembly established transitional "organizational laws" that gradually morphed into the **Constitution of 1875**, effectively founding the Third Republic. This constitution created:

1. A President of the Republic, elected by the legislature, with a seven-year term.
2. A bicameral legislature: the Senate (indirectly elected) and the Chamber of Deputies (directly elected).
3. Executive powers that included naming ministers, yet these ministers were accountable to the legislative majority.

While monarchists intended these arrangements as temporary, it quickly became permanent, for the monarchy never reunited around a single candidate.

---

3. Institutionalizing the Republic

MacMahon and the 16 May Crisis (1877)

Marshal MacMahon, conservative at heart, clashed with the republican majority in the Chamber of Deputies. In May 1877, he dismissed the moderate republican prime minister Jules Simon, appointing a more conservative government. The Chamber responded with defiance, leading to a standoff known as the **16 May Crisis**. MacMahon dissolved the Chamber, hoping new elections would yield a royalist or conservative majority. Instead, republicans triumphed even more decisively. Sensing the impossibility of resisting the popular will, MacMahon resigned in 1879.

This crisis solidified the principle that the executive must align with the parliamentary majority—an important milestone for parliamentary democracy. After MacMahon's departure, Jules Grévy, a committed republican, became President, and republican leaders like **Léon Gambetta** guided legislation.

Republican "Moral Order" and Social Reforms

Republicans undertook measures to anchor the regime's legitimacy. They removed monarchist symbols from public spaces, insisted on the national motto "Liberté, Égalité, Fraternité," and fostered a patriotic narrative stressing 1789's legacy. They also advanced free public schooling, championed by **Jules Ferry**, who as Minister of Public Instruction (beginning in 1879) enacted laws making primary education compulsory, free, and secular. This aimed to reduce Catholic Church influence and cultivate a civic-minded citizenry loyal to the Republic.

Church-State Relations

Throughout the 1880s, tensions flared with the Catholic Church, which favored monarchism or at least limited republican power. Ferry's secular education laws restricted religious instruction in state schools, and congregations faced constraints. Many conservative Catholics saw this as anti-clerical oppression. Meanwhile, republican leaders considered Church meddling a threat to democracy, reflecting the lasting conflict over religion sparked by the Revolution and Napoleonic Concordat.

---

4. Colonial Expansion and International Position

Motivations for a Colonial Empire

In the late 19th century, republican France embarked on renewed **colonial expansion**. Reasons included:

1. **Economic Interests**: Entrepreneurs sought raw materials, overseas markets, and profitable concessions.
2. **National Prestige**: Post-1871, acquiring colonies was seen as compensation for the lost provinces of Alsace-Lorraine and a demonstration of France's global stature.
3. **Civilizing Mission**: Influenced by Enlightenment ideals and paternalistic attitudes, many French believed in spreading "modern civilization" to Africa and Asia.

Thus, the Third Republic established or intensified control over regions in Africa (e.g., Senegal, Ivory Coast, Madagascar), Indochina (present-day Vietnam, Cambodia, Laos), and extended influence in North Africa beyond Algeria.

Diplomatic Situation in Europe

France's primary foreign policy concern was Germany, now unified under the Prussian-led empire. After 1871, tensions remained high over Alsace-Lorraine, with France longing to recover these "lost provinces." However, direct confrontation seemed impossible, as Germany possessed a robust military advantage. French leaders pursued alliances to counterbalance Germany, forging eventually the **Franco-Russian Alliance (1894)**. Meanwhile, relations with Britain fluctuated, though by the end of the century shared colonial rivalries gave way to cautious cooperation, laying groundwork for the later **Entente Cordiale** (1904).

Expositions Universelles

In an effort to showcase industrial and cultural achievements, the Third Republic organized grand exhibitions—**Expositions Universelles**—in Paris (notably in 1878, 1889, and 1900). These events displayed France's technological progress, colonial acquisitions, and artistic innovations, promoting the idea that the Republic was a beacon of modernity and refinement.

---

5. Domestic Challenges

Workers' Movements and Political Socialism

The Industrial Revolution advanced, particularly in mining, textiles, and metallurgy, enlarging the urban working class. Social inequality and harsh conditions led to the growth of **socialist** ideologies. French Marxists, inspired by the First International (founded in 1864), formed political clubs and labor unions. While divided into factions (Guesdists vs. Blanquists vs. reformist socialists), they all pressed for better wages, reduced working hours, and legal recognition of unions.

By the 1880s, republican politicians like **Léon Gambetta** recognized the need to co-opt moderate workers via limited reforms—some improved labor conditions or recognized unions in certain industries. However, the radical left continued pushing for deeper economic restructuring, forming a vocal minority in the Chamber of Deputies.

The Boulangist Movement (1887–1889)

General **Georges Boulanger** emerged as a nationalist figure who capitalized on popular discontent with parliamentary corruption, the humiliating memory of 1871, and calls for revenge against Germany. Embraced by monarchists, Bonapartists, and some radical republicans, Boulanger threatened to overthrow the regime in a coup. His fame soared in 1888–1889, winning by-elections on a platform promising to "dissolve the Chamber, revise the Constitution, and avenge the fatherland."

Ultimately, Boulanger lost his nerve. Instead of seizing power, he hesitated. The government prosecuted him for treason, and he fled into exile, committing suicide in 1891. The "Boulangist Crisis" highlighted the fragility of the Republic—mass political movements could challenge parliamentary institutions. But its failure also reinforced the resilience of republican structures and the electorate's wariness of authoritarian solutions.

---

6. The Dreyfus Affair and the Triumph of Republican Ideals

Background of the Affair

The **Dreyfus Affair (1894–1906)** rocked France's social and political fabric. In 1894, Captain **Alfred Dreyfus**, a Jewish officer in the French army, was accused of passing military secrets to Germany. Convicted in a secret court martial with flimsy evidence, he was sent to Devil's Island in French Guiana. Over time, evidence emerged that the real traitor was another officer. High-ranking army officials covered up the truth, forging documents to maintain Dreyfus's guilt.

The Nation Divided

Revelations about Dreyfus's probable innocence triggered a national uproar. The affair split France into two camps:

1. **Dreyfusards**: Republicans, intellectuals, socialists, and moderate Catholics who demanded justice and a retrial, championing evidence over blind loyalty to the army. The novelist Émile Zola's **"J'Accuse...!"** open letter was a rallying cry for this side.
2. **Anti-Dreyfusards**: Military conservatives, many Catholics, monarchists, and nationalist leagues who viewed the matter as an attack on the honor of the army and were often influenced by anti-Semitic sentiments.

The press and political clubs fueled intense debate, at times erupting in riots. The affair laid bare deep-seated prejudices (anti-Semitism) and stark disagreements about the Republic's values of equality and rule of law.

Dreyfus's Vindication

After protracted legal battles, Dreyfus was retried and eventually exonerated in 1906. The affair had colossal impacts:

- **Strengthening of Republican Institutions**: The government overcame infiltration by reactionary elements in the army and reaffirmed the primacy of civilian authority and individual rights.
- **Secular Emphasis**: Many Republicans associated the anti-Dreyfus stance with clerical and nationalist extremes. Thus, the case reinforced the drive for further separation of Church and State (culminating in the 1905 law).
- **Free Press and Civil Liberties**: Despite heated polemics, the affair underscored the importance of free debate and journalism in shaping public opinion, cementing a robust if fractious political culture.

---

7. Society and Culture at the Fin de Siècle

Intellectual Currents

The late 19th century, often termed **fin de siècle**, saw a flourishing of French arts and letters. Writers like **Guy de Maupassant**, **Émile Zola**, and the younger generation of symbolist poets (e.g., **Mallarmé**, **Verlaine**, **Rimbaud**) probed social realities, moral ambiguities, and the complexities of modern life. Naturalism (Zola) stressed the influence of environment and heredity on characters, reflecting the period's interest in scientific determinism.

Scientific and Technological Advances

France contributed significantly to the era's scientific breakthroughs. Figures like **Louis Pasteur** pioneered germ theory, transforming medicine and public health. Innovations in electricity, communications, and transportation further accelerated industrial growth. Engineers built iconic structures, including the **Eiffel Tower** (completed in 1889 for the Exposition Universelle), symbolizing technical prowess and marking the centennial of the Revolution.

Urban and Rural Life

Rapid industrial expansion fueled urban migration. Major cities like Paris, Lyon, and Marseille swelled with factory workers, artisans, and service-sector employees. Meanwhile, rural regions modernized slowly, with peasant communities maintaining traditional lifestyles but adopting some mechanized tools. Education reforms gradually reduced illiteracy and introduced patriotic narratives to unify a population still bearing regional dialects and customs.

---

8. The Political Landscape by 1900

Multiple Republican Factions

By 1900, the Third Republic had weathered numerous crises—Commune, royalist plots, Boulangism, Dreyfus—and remained standing. Its supporters fragmented into various republican groupings:

1. **Radical Republicans**: Advocated strong secular policies, expansion of social welfare, and further democratization.
2. **Moderate Republicans (Opportunists)**: Preferred pragmatic governance, free-market economics, and gradual reform, exemplified by figures like Jules Ferry.
3. **Socialists**: Gaining ground among urban workers, calling for economic justice and state intervention to protect labor.

Monarchists, Bonapartists, and Catholic conservatives still had representation, but they no longer posed an imminent threat to the Republic's survival.

Colonial Competition and National Pride

French colonial holdings expanded in Africa (e.g., the scramble for territories like Madagascar, West Africa) and Southeast Asia (French Indochina). While these endeavors enriched some industrialists and created illusions of global prestige, they also led to local resistance, administrative complexities, and rivalries with Britain and other powers. At home, colonial conquests sometimes boosted national pride, offsetting the bitterness of 1871. Nonetheless, the moral and financial costs of empire would become topics of debate within the republic.

Toward a New Century

By the eve of the 20th century, France was a predominantly rural nation but undergoing steady industrialization. The Republic championed universal schooling, secular institutions, and a patriotic mission to avenge the lost provinces if the opportunity arose—though official policy remained cautious. The humiliations of the Franco-Prussian War lingered, influencing diplomatic alignments such as the Franco-Russian Alliance, while domestic politics revolved around reconciling social demands, managing labor unrest, and consolidating parliamentary traditions.

---

9. The End of the 19th Century

Enduring Republican Identity

Despite repeated threats, the Third Republic proved remarkably resilient. By the 1890s, monarchy restoration seemed unlikely, with the republican model deeply entrenched in public schools, local governments, and national symbols (the Marseillaise, the tricolor flag). Regular elections, expanded civil liberties (albeit limited for women), and a vibrant press nourished a civic consciousness. Although conservative Catholicism remained influential in parts of rural France, the regime's secular orientation persisted, culminating in the 1905 **law separating Church and State** (slightly beyond 1900, but largely shaped by the late 19th-century discourse).

Social and Cultural Modernity

The final decades of the 19th century witnessed an intellectual and artistic effervescence. The Impressionist movement (Monet, Renoir, Degas) revolutionized painting, capturing fleeting impressions of modern life. Writers and thinkers from across Europe gravitated to Paris, the "capital of the 19th century," as historian Walter Benjamin later termed it. Technological wonders—from the Eiffel Tower to modern transport—symbolized faith in progress. But the period also harbored undercurrents of anxiety, as the Dreyfus Affair revealed. Rising nationalism, social inequality, and political polarization foreshadowed the complexities of the next century.

---

10. Conclusion

By the close of the 19th century, France had journeyed from the chaos of the Franco-Prussian War and the bitter aftermath of the Paris Commune to a relatively stable **Third Republic**. Surviving attempted monarchist restorations, internal revolts, and the Boulanger and Dreyfus crises, the Republic gradually entrenched itself, expanding public education, strengthening civilian control over the military, and forging a sense of unified national identity—albeit one laced with tensions over secularism, colonial expansion, and social reform.

This chapter concludes our broad survey of French history before modern times. Across twenty chapters, we have seen France evolve from prehistoric settlements, through the Gauls, Roman conquest, medieval kingdoms, the Capetian rise, Valois and Bourbon monarchies, revolutionary upheavals, Napoleonic ambition, and the eventual Republican framework. By 1900, France stood at the threshold of a new century, shaped by the legacy of revolution, empire, and republican ideals—a complex tapestry that would continue to evolve in the decades to come.

Although we halt our narrative here, the reader can trace many of these 19th-century currents—nationalism, secularization, industrial transformation, social movements—straight into the major events of the 20th century. For now, we conclude with France at the dawn of a new era, **a republican nation** grappling with the modern world, having traversed a centuries-long journey that laid the foundation for its enduring cultural, political, and social identity.

Printed in Great Britain
by Amazon